D0677104

AGAINST THE STREAM

AGAINST ᴛʜᴇ STREAM

Growing Up Where Hitler Used to Live

Anna Elisabeth Rosmus

translated from the German by
Imogen von Tannenberg

© 2002 Anna Elisabeth Rosmus

Published in Columbia, South Carolina, by the
University of South Carolina Press

Manufactured in the United States of America

06 05 04 03 02   5 4 3 2 1

Library of Congress Cataloging-in-Publication Data

Rosmus, Anna.
  [Was ich denke. English]
  Against the stream : growing up where Hitler used to live / Anna Elisabeth
Rosmus ; translated from the German by Imogen von Tannenberg.
    p. cm.
  ISBN 1-57003-490-7 (alk. paper)
  1. Rosmus, Anna. 2. Women—Germany—Passau—Biography. 3. Passau
(Germany)—Biography. 4. National socialism—Germany—Passau. 5. World
War, 1939–1945—Atrocities. 6. Holocaust, Jewish (1939–1945)—Germany
Passau (Landkreis) I. Tannenberg, Imogen von. II. Title.
  DD901.P (Passau)
  943'.355087'092—dc21   2002009358

Special thanks go to Scott Evan Burgess, whose talents helped shape the final
form of this translation.

To those who instilled in me the desire to search for the truth

CONTENTS

CONTENTS

PREFACE

PASSAU, MY HOMETOWN, IS located at Germany's border with Austria and the Czech Republic. Many people in America know Passau as a baroque Eden on the banks of three rivers, an ancient bishop's seat. They come as tourists and love it for its beauty. But how many people know that Adolf Hitler and Adolf Eichmann lived there? How many people know that, in the spring of 1920, long before the Nazi movement, a citizen of Passau officially called for anti-Jewish boycotts, Aryanization, concentration camps, and genocide? There was a time when I didn't know about any of this. And I grew up in Passau.

Ever since I discovered the truth about Passau's past, I have tried to take as many people as possible behind the scenes of this scenic city. I tell them that after centuries of deadly anti-Semitism and four more centuries of Jews being formally banned from the city, it wasn't until 1871 that Jews were granted basic civil rights—including the right to resettle in the city. At the turn of the century the first Jews did return to Passau. They were merchants from abroad who started businesses and opened small shops. At that same time Adolf Hitler also lived in Passau with his family. His father was an employee at the local customs office. His older brother went to the city's most reputable secondary school, where Heinrich Himmler's father was a teacher. Adolf's younger brother Edmund was born in Passau. Ernst Kaltenbrunner, the chief of the Nazi security police, grew up nearby, and from Passau he organized the annexation of Austria—together with Adolf Eichmann. I would only later discover the disturbing details of the role Passau played in the Nazi era.

At the end of the Second World War a few prisoners who had escaped from one of the city's concentration camps led the Americans to the Passau I sub-camp. The Americans liberated the few remaining survivors of those long years of brutality. Passau II, the Americans discovered, had quite obviously been evacuated in a panic and the prisoners massacred. The inmates of Passau III, a mobile unit responsible primarily for defusing bombs, were found murdered in bomb craters, their bodies used as filling material.

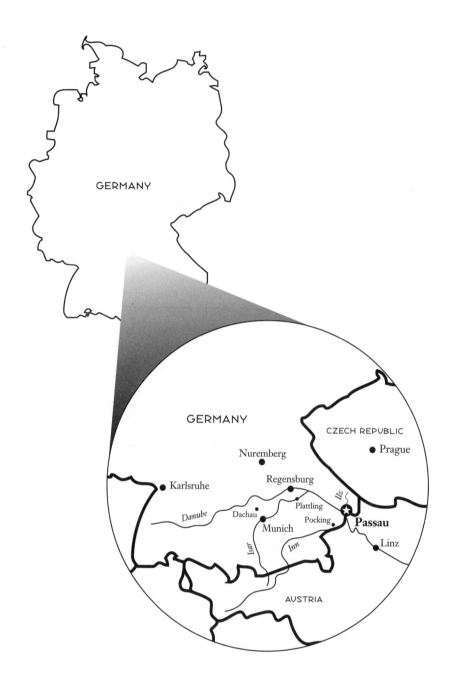

Map of Germany, with detail showing the location of Passau at the confluence of the rivers Ilz, Inn, and Danube, plus the locations of the concentration camps Dachau, Plattling, and Pocking

I have never argued Passau is a uniquely evil place, nor that all who lived there throughout the Nazi era have blood on their hands. What I do believe, and what I will never stop saying, is that my hometown provides a striking symbol of Germany's Nazi past, and may have something invaluable to teach us, a lesson that we cannot afford to ignore. Throughout the many years of my research into Passau's past, whenever I discovered something new the initial reaction from the city officials was always the same: "More lies." Later, when my findings would be proven true they would say: "Yes, but that all happened a long time ago," and "Anyway, was it really that terrible?" Somehow the victims were always forgotten. This book is intended to honor their memory.

AGAINST THE STREAM

Prologue

DO YOU LOVE GERMANY?

SHORTLY AFTER THE BIRTH of my second daughter, Salome, I received a call asking if I would be interested in contributing an essay to an anthology titled *Do You Love Germany?* The payment was ridiculously small, but quite a few interesting people had already agreed to contribute, among them the journalist Henryk Broder, Monika Griefahn from Greenpeace, and the German-Jewish author Grete Weill. I was told it would only have to be about ten pages.

Ten pages were not a lot, but as I had never really asked myself this question before I couldn't think of an answer—at least not right away. And the thought of sitting down to write with a baby and a toddler to care for wasn't exactly appealing either. But I was tempted. And so I agreed.

While changing diapers and during feedings, while cooking and cleaning, I thought about my relationship to Germany. I thought about myself and "the Germans," about my recently published book *Resistance and Persecution in Passau from 1933 to 1939* and the various reactions to it.

When the anthology came out the Passau city councilman, Franz Mader, felt he had been wronged, and he took me to court on the grounds of libel. But I was not going to sit quietly and leave things to fate. I called the small, alternative Passau newspaper, the *Passauer Aktuelle Zeitung*, and asked whether they might be interested in this case. They asked me to come by immediately and to bring a copy of the complaint with me. A few days later a scandal erupted: the complaint made the front page.

In 1986, in the fall issue of the New York magazine *Aufbau*, Ulrich Chaussy wrote of the incident:

> Here is a man who will go to any length to publicly discredit Anna Rosmus and to greatly impede her work: he is Franz Mader, fifty-five years old, CSU city councilman, currently employed in the deanery of the Catholic Church.
>
> He was in the audience during a forum in which Anna Rosmus disturbed the flawless image that had been presented of the Passau clergy

when she spoke about the cases of two priests who had denounced the Jewish clothes salesman, Fabian Heitzner, to the Gestapo. Franz Mader's personal record of the minutes (*Protokoll*) of this forum provides the basis for various press releases published in the Diocese Paper (*Passauer Bistumsblatt*) and the *Passauer Neue Presse*, in which Anna Rosmus is accused of being the source of "obvious untruths," "filthy slander," and even "outrageous libel."

I was twenty-four years old and had recently been forced to discontinue my studies as a result of expecting my second child during the semester in "this Germany." I had prevailed in another lawsuit against the City of Passau dealing with my right to access "public" archives. I had become the recipient of extraordinary honors, including the prestigious Geschwister-Scholl Award, named after the Scholl siblings who organized the movement the White Rose (*Weiße Rose*) to resist the Nazis and were later denounced and executed.

I was a German living in Germany. But did that make me a "typical German?" A few days later I sat down and began to put my thoughts on paper. It was late in the evening and my husband was reading. I had some time—a few hours at least. I wrote:

Sometimes I have the feeling that an entire town has conspired against me. I was repeatedly told files were missing, on loan for years, or vanished somewhere on their way through the "official channels." In my homeland I continue to be harassed, denounced, and hunted down simply because I dare to ask questions about its recent history. And so I ask myself: Can I honestly say that I love a country whose people simply can't deal with their own past? Can I feel at home in a land where my audiences have to be protected by police during public appearances because of bomb threats? Can I feel safe if the phone is ringing off the hook with threatening calls, just because I'm writing a book about some Jews in Passau?

There are people in this country who say they're sorry I wasn't alive in the Middle Ages. Back then, they say, I would have been drowned or burned at the stake. Others would like to see me gassed in the concentration camp, quartered, and chopped to pieces, so that I would finally keep my "stinking Jew-mouth shut." I have asked myself: what kind of people are these who refer to me as "Jew-whore" (*Judenhure*) and "filthy pig" (*Drecksau*) because I am researching the current whereabouts of some of Passau's Jews? What kind of country is "this Germany" where I'm asked whether I am programming my own daughter for

2

the concentration camp simply because I name her Salome? What kind of attitude did those people have who accused me of dealing with "such repulsive scum, such disgusting miscreants" as Jews? People whose mentality expresses itself in statements such as, "Considering how much money the Jews have received in reparations, you'd think they'd be satisfied with the few lives they had to sacrifice for it." And what might the type of people ultimately be capable of who threatened to kill me because I had helped young people from all over the world document the history of a concentration camp?

When the CSU city councilman Franz Mader was asked to retract his slanders against me, his lawyer simply stated that his client saw no reason to do so. As an employee of the church he was also a representative of the people. I have asked myself: does he speak for the people? In the elections for city council that followed this incident his popularity actually rose as he rose in rank. He was appointed local heritage custodian (*Heimatpfleger*) of the City of Passau. What, exactly, is all this "representative" of? And should such a person be deserving of our respect?

A country made up of men such as Martin Hirsch and Hans Lamm would deserve to be respected, a nation with such qualities as theirs would deserve to be loved. When I realized what it was that I valued so much in people like these I also realized what I found most lacking in Germany. Why do so few speak out against the often oppressive, bullying bureaucracy? Why are so many people so hung up on the trivial rules and regulations set down by the state on how to live a conventional and respectable German life, instead of concentrating on the essential things and trying to become a better person? Why are so many people afraid to take responsibility for their actions, and why is it that a simple act of obedience toward authority frequently turns into a kind of blind faith in authority? Why does a person's uniform or official title mean more than their character to most Germans? I am worried about the thoughtlessness: how can anyone think about the murdered victims of Auschwitz without asking where they came from, who took them there, and what kind of mentality was responsible for their deaths?

I so much would like to live among a people (*Volk*) that does not fear or suppress the truth, a nation that admits to its past mistakes. I would so much like to live in a nation where somebody who thinks "against the stream" can be an adversary but not necessarily the enemy. I would like to live among people who can take criticism, among people who will try to right their wrongs instead of trying to hide them. I would like to live in a country whose official representatives help to expose dangers and fight against them instead of pretending they don't exist. In my view the sovereignty of a nation reveals itself in precisely these attributes, and not in the question of where a territorial authority recognizes its limits. I would like to live among people who see each person as an individual, and I would like to see each human being be allowed to be just that, a human being. Why are terms such as "nation," "religion," "heritage," and "prosperity" so significant? I would like it if people could simply be there for each other. It doesn't really matter what we might call such a nation, as long as that nation measures the value of its citizens according to these standards. That is the country I would like to live in.

But since such a nation does not exist at present, and since, like everybody else, I must remain a citizen of some nation, I will continue to live in Germany, despite all its negative traits: I value our constitution because it grants the broadest freedoms possible, because it allows for diversity, and because it puts few constraints on its people. I am grateful for this constitution because it provides institutions and avenues that can be used to control and ensure the fairness of how it is applied. Whenever it is violated it is usually possible for even a single individual to defend him or herself. If I, as a mere student, can sue a city and succeed, then this serves as a sign for me that this nation basically works.

Of course I have learned that even in this nation being right doesn't necessarily ensure justice. I have experienced firsthand what it means to be denounced as an enemy of the constitution for the "crime" of pointing out truths that are not officially recognized. And I have learned that in certain regions freedom of the press exists in theory more than in reality. And yet it is in exactly this context that I have experienced how reassuring and encouraging it can be when people come together spontaneously and begin to assist those who have suffered an injustice. I have found support from the clergy and from Communists, from victims of the National Socialist (NS) prosecution and from former NS perpetrators, from people who lived through the past and from their descendants, from individuals and from institutions. When the local press tried to pretend I didn't exist, when I was not allowed to publish any statements outlining and explaining my own point of view, there were many others from the national press, from radio and television, and especially reporters from the magazine *Der Spiegel*, and the two largest national newspapers, the Munich *Süddeutsche Zeitung*, and the Hamburg *Die Zeit*, who stepped in. Their reports generated much sympathy for my cause and helped form lasting alliances. It was through actions like these that I was able to feel as though I was no longer fighting, alone and isolated, against an overwhelming force. Just knowing that any future attacks against me would not go completely unanswered has given me a sense of security.

Soon I came into contact with people who thought like me, who were engaged in similar kinds of work, and who had experiences similar to mine. I've learned a great deal from these (usually older) people and would not want to trade a single one of these encounters for the world, even if the experiences we discussed were bitter ones. A flood of new contacts came in after I received the Geschwister-Scholl Award. Almost overnight my house became a "port of call" for many Germans, and sometimes I was shocked to find myself listening to what amounted to personal confessions. Many people saw me as a confidant and a symbol of courage and strength.

And this despite the fact that I had never planned on playing the revolutionary. It was never my intention to become a rebel; I didn't want to quarrel with anyone. I had never been politically active and it had never been my ambition to make waves. I never wanted to disturb anybody's peace or to destroy anyone's image . . . nevertheless I became an outsider in the eyes of many people for the mere reason that one of my topics had to do with Passau. What kept me going was my conviction that justice was being violated here, and that the truth was being deliberately falsified. My determination to discover the truth led to many negative experiences. I wouldn't want to have missed any of them. It was high time I started learning.

I wrote into the early morning hours. The manuscript was complete. I had described in broad strokes how my work had been received. I wanted to thank the people who had assisted me in my search for the truth, but at the same time I didn't want to withhold mentioning the enormous pressures I had been subjected to. And I wanted to encourage all those who were toying with the idea of exploring similar unconventional avenues by stating frankly how much help I had received from the outside when I had first left my nest and begun exploring.

Chapter 1

AGAINST THE STREAM

I HAVE BEEN THINKING "against the stream" for quite some time now. I tend to rub people the wrong way because my beliefs are not befitting of a "conventional" young woman, and because many conventional people simply don't understand much of what I believe—yet.

But my life and beliefs weren't always so controversial. I was born in 1960, in Passau, a small city in Lower Bavaria (*Niederbayern*), Germany. Both my parents were teachers. In 1956, before they met, they were transferred to the elementary school in Auerbach, where they grew to like each other. It was at school that they literally came together. The students, noticing this, would sometimes make well-meaning remarks to each other about the curious crease in my mother's elegant skirt: "Where did *that* come from?" they would ask. A short time later my parents were engaged to be married.

My father's family were displaced persons, expatriated from Silesia; his father was murdered at the end of the Second World War. His mother, brother, and sister had initially fled to Lower Bavaria with the help of the Red Cross, where they worked as nurses and medical assistants in a field hospital. When my father was released from a French POW camp he went to Straubing in the hope of finding his relatives. He was already enrolled in law school in Silesia, but because he had no money he had to go to work as a farmhand. He learned to use an ox-drawn plow and to harvest crops. When the situation in postwar Germany had finally calmed down a bit, he became a teacher. It was the only course of study that did not require any tuition fees.

My mother was born in Passau. Her father was an Austrian who served in the First World War, where he was exposed to poison gas, the effects of which he died from a few years later. My mother was the youngest of four children and only nine days old when her father died. Her mother was forced to work, because as a German widow she was not entitled to social security from the Austrian government. During the day she worked as a doctor's assistant; in the mornings and evenings she worked as a maid, as the money from her day job wasn't enough to support the family. She left the house at five every morning—after she was done bathing my mother and braiding her hair to get her ready for kindergarten. In the spring and the fall, when the carnival was in town, she also sewed the outfits worn by the circus monkeys.

All four children ended up getting some form of higher education. The three brothers attended the high school for humanities (*Humanistische Gymnasium*), the *Leopoldinum*. All three also went to the Catholic seminary. Two planned to become priests, the other a monk. All three went to war instead. Only the youngest returned. My mother remembers how my grandmother cried and prayed constantly during that time. Mother was fifteen years old and attended a music and fine-arts high school (*Musische Gymnasium*). She played piano and violin and planned to become a home economics teacher. She was very well behaved, although she would sometimes cut school and take a walk in the park with her boyfriend. The school had forbidden its students to take dance classes, but my mother was allowed to attend anyway after my grandmother had told the school director that education was a private matter and if a mother gives her permission it was not the school's place to deny it. A few years before, while the school was under Nazi administration and set up as a training place for future Party elite, the students were not permitted to attend Holy Mass. My mother went anyway. My grandmother would not have had it any other way. She told the school officials that my mother would only come to school if she were allowed to pray on a regular basis and attend Holy Mass.

I was unaware of all of this at the time. I too was a "good girl" who, shortly after having graduated from high school, had married my former math teacher and was all ready to begin my studies at Passau University. I planned to become a teacher, so I could teach foreign students.

Chapter 2

THE IMAGE OF PASSAU

MANFRED PFISTER, THE PROFESSOR and literary critic, writes in the travel magazine *Merian:*

> Passau is a sleepy town, so much so that it managed for a long time to avoid making headlines: only the seasonal floods of its three rivers or the occasional small scandal of a certain delicate or, perhaps, political nature had managed to cause a gentle "rustling of the leaves" in a few major papers. The city, located at the easternmost edge of the country, has since attained a degree of notoriety and symbolic power reminiscent of *Kotzebues Krähwinkel.*

In 1975, the conservative, Bavarian Christian Social Union (CSU) moved its Political Ash Wednesday meeting from nearby Vilshofen to the Nibelungen Hall (*Nibelungenhalle*) in Passau. At the same time, another political spectacle was about to enter the picture, in a kind of counter-production of power. It would take place not in the "Great House" located at the edge of the *Exerzienplatz*, which was built by the Nazis and is a paragon of ugliness, but instead in the "Small House," which lies in the shadow of the cathedral hill (*Domberg*) and City Hall (*Rathaus*). The "Small House" had been the local executioner's house. The topic of both events: "Why is the spirit of the CSU felt nowhere as strongly as in Passau?"

It was through the subsequent publicity that Passau became the center of major media events within just a few years. It is now known for its [un]Holy Trinity of "Clergy, CSU-two-thirds-majority, and Conservative press"—a combination, which, according to some in the major newspapers, has transformed the city into the unofficial capital of German provincialism.

Many people have accused me personally, both in public and in private, of being to blame for all of this. You see, I was thinking "against the stream." It was suggested more than once that I should make my home and, especially, my living, elsewhere. If I had to think differently from the others, they said, why couldn't I at least keep my mouth shut? Manfred Pfister characterized the situation in *Merian:* "She is a painful thorn in the side of the city, particularly because she comes from a respectable middle-class family. And if that were not enough, the fact that she 'dirtied her own nest' (*ihre Nestbeschmutzung*) was rewarded by her being honored with the Geschwister-Scholl Award in the distant capital of Munich."

It all began innocently enough. In 1979 my German teacher suggested that I participate in a Europe-wide essay contest. The essay only had to be ten pages, and he even offered to let me substitute this assignment for one of our normal oral reports and grade it with an "A+." Normally I'd have to work my butt off for days to earn an "A+" in German. So I agreed. The following weekend at lunch I told my uncle about the contest and asked if he had any ideas for a subject. He immediately suggested the title "Concepts of Internal and External Freedom." I could start with the death of Socrates, who had chosen to drink the cup of hemlock instead of betraying his convictions. I could mention Jesus. Jesus had been a rebel who died for his belief. Socrates. Sure. I had read about him in Latin class. And I also knew that Jesus had been a martyr and that he had ultimately been delivered into the hands of his executioners; but a rebel? How had my uncle come up with that idea? I had never heard such a thing. It didn't make sense to me, although my uncle was himself a priest and had been teaching at various universities for decades.

I decided to ask him what he meant. Jesus had always been very gentle and obedient, hadn't he? My uncle did not find this funny at all. He quickly looked up from his plate and said sharply, "Obedient? Jesus was a rebel! He went into the temple and he pushed over the merchants' tables; he didn't observe the Sabbath, at least not in the eyes of the scribes. He chose to heal on the Sabbath, even though all work was strictly forbidden on that day. Jesus was not sentenced to death because he was obedient; he died because he was a rebel!"

The stories I had always heard never interpreted Jesus this way. But somehow my uncle sounded convincing. Perhaps I should read up a bit about this, I thought. While we were on the subject I decided to ask my uncle what other types of things I should include in my essay. He suggested I mention the year 1789, the year of the French Revolution, and 1848, when Karl Marx published the *Communist Manifesto*, dates that marked the triumph of civil liberties. . . . And then, last but not least, there was the year 1949, when the German Constitution was ratified, a document that would make it impossible for another system of injustice like the Nazis' to ever arise in Germany again.

I was fascinated by my uncle's idea of writing about concepts of freedom; we'd never learned anything about such things in school. And the material he had spontaneously suggested was anything but orthodox. I went straight to the library the very next day to begin doing research.

The essay could be no more than ten pages long, and it didn't take me long to write it. I received my "A+" and then turned my attention to the all-important exit exams (*Abitur*). I had just completed the final written exams when the assistant principal, Helmut von Baumgarten, stopped me in the hallway and asked me into his office. I had no idea why and immediately thought the worst. He closed the door behind us and said: "Congratulations!" Strange, I thought, since I had not yet passed the oral exams and was certain that the written tests could not have been corrected yet. What was this all about? He grinned and handed me a letter. I had won first prize in the essay contest. This was the last thing I had expected. But there it was, in black and white. Herr von Baumgarten started laughing and told me, "You're going to Paris." I stared at the letter and could not believe my luck. There must have been many other excellent essays. Concepts of Europe, Concepts of Freedom; it must have been my choice of subjects. . . .

When I came home my parents had already sat down to lunch. I joined them at the table and asked if they remembered the contest. Then I told them that I had won first prize. My father looked up for a moment and teased: "Well, I guess the others must have been even worse than you!"

I'll never forget this comment as long as I live. I was brought up not to be arrogant about success, and my father never particularly heaped praise upon me; but did he have to be so dismissive? "Even worse than you!" My mother tried to ease the tension a bit: "Have something to eat first," she said.

How was I to tell them about Paris? I had just turned twenty, so they could not really prevent me from going. If they tried, I would insist I be allowed to go. I would travel alone to Paris, on a ticket I didn't have to ask anyone to buy for me; I had earned it because I had written a good essay! My parents couldn't stop me, and neither could my fiancé.

After lunch I told my parents exactly what I had won: I would be going to France for ten days, together with the winners from other countries; we would all be going to Brittany and Normandy; there was to be a reception at the city hall in Paris—and everything would be paid for. My father was silent, and my mother simply asked: "To Paris . . . all by yourself . . . ?"

I completed the oral part of my exams in the subject "Catholic theology," using parts of my essay for my answers, and received an "A"—even though I had quoted, among others, Marx, while speaking on the topic of "Proofs of God."

Shortly after exams, we celebrated graduation. When the assistant principal asked for volunteers to give the graduation speech, some of those who were not exactly the stars of the class raised their hands. I was surprised, yet relieved. "Good," I thought. "At least it's not me again!" Some people made a point of not coming to the ceremony, as they considered it too establishmentarian. Others protested the ceremony by planning to show up dressed in jeans and T-shirts. In the end a committee had written the speech. I arrived in the morning, accompanied by my parents, just like a good girl should, to receive my certificate: I was the only one who had dressed up. My white, barebacked cocktail dress earned me some boos (*Pfiffe*) as well as a smattering of applause. It wasn't the first time something like that had happened, though. I felt comfortable the way I was. The thing that made me feel miserable was the graduation speech—which was given in all of our names.

I was never a perfect student and I was certainly no teacher's pet. But the words that came out of my colleague's mouth were shameful. It was an immature and not very amusing attempt to badmouth the school. There were, of course, many things that deserved criticizing, but the criticism should have taken a different form. There was not one word acknowledging any of the teachers who had sacrificed countless hours for us, who had been there for us, and who had tolerated more than a few of our pranks and idiosyncrasies. To fail to mention these facts on graduation day seemed to me more than simply in bad taste. I felt ashamed for our class. I considered walking up there and adding my own postscript. But my seat was right in the middle of the row, and a lot of people would have been disturbed if I had shoved my way up to the front. Anyway, who knows if anybody would have even let me say anything, after that kind of speech. It was not in my nature to jeer her, and for one single person to stand up and demonstratively walk out of the hall would not have been too impressive either. I was still considering what to do when the speech ended. I could see the dismay in some my friends' faces; they were as ashamed as I was. But nobody had gotten up, no one had protested.

A few minutes later we received our diplomas, and the best students were awarded prizes. My award was mentioned as well. As I was walking to the front, I was still thinking about how I could salvage the situation. There were some dirty looks and more comments about my being an establishment sell-out, and before I knew it I had my diploma in my hands and the guidance counselor was "recording the image for me and my posterity" in an official photograph. In spite of this dreadful speech! I didn't know what to say, and so I said nothing. This is another moment that will stay with me for the rest of my life: I was silent when I should have spoken up. I was silent because of my own insecurities. I didn't protest, neither visibly nor audibly, because I had wasted too much time thinking about what to do. I should have jumped out of my seat and stormed the stage—regardless of what anybody might have thought. I should have distanced myself from the speech, for the sake of justice, and for the sake of my own credibility.

That's when I vowed to myself: never again will you be silent if something has to be said. You will open your mouth and protest whenever and wherever you find injustice.

A few weeks later I was on my way to France. I was curious to know how it would go. We were a very mixed group, with a great variety of interests. Some of the participants really impressed me: they were a lot more knowledgeable about many things than I was. Two of them had written essays on economics subjects I had never even heard about; another was an expert in international politics and knew all the key dates by heart. They were all younger than I. Some of them were very well-versed and worldly, others a bit crude. Each was fluent in at least two languages, and even that was still considered a bit lacking. Jean-Claude, our advisor, had to ask me repeatedly for help with the translations, mostly from French to Italian and vice versa. We were going to Normandy, where the Allied forces had landed in 1944 to liberate Europe from National Socialism. Up to this point I knew next to nothing about this historic event. We gave interviews to French reporters, toured Versailles, and had tons of fun. While others were busy flirting, falling in love, and swapping rooms, I bought my bridal veil. At the end of the trip some of us decided to participate in the next competition in the hope that we might win a second time and get to see each other again.

When I returned home my sister and my parents were waiting for me with their suitcases packed. We were going on vacation to Italy together, one last time as a family, before I was to be married.

As my wedding date began to draw nearer, I started to get cold feet, as did my fiancé. But we had already made the announcement and sent out the invitations. People in town had been gossiping about us for various reasons: because yet again, a teacher was marrying a former student, because I was allowed to marry in the cathedral, something which, as was dutifully reported in the tabloid press, even the Prince of Thurn and Taxis had not been permitted to do! In order to avoid a scandal, we did get married after all, in a conventional ceremony.

It was September, the pressures of schoolwork were behind me . . . and I was bored out of my mind. My husband was working and I was not used to simply sitting around. The semester wasn't set to start until November. After a few days my father came home from school and brought me the paperwork for yet another writing competition. He chuckled: "Could this be something for you? This time I'm sure you know absolutely nothing about the topic!" I looked at the announcement and read the title without much enthusiasm: "The Prewar Years in My Hometown," organized by the Körber Foundation in Hamburg. No, this was not for me. My knowledge of history was not outstanding. Sure, I had received an "A" on my diploma (*im Abiturzeugnis*), but I knew next to nothing about the prewar years. I had very little knowledge about the war and none at all about wartime events in my hometown. The only thing I knew about Passau was a little bit of medieval history; in elementary school we had learned about the Plague. We had also visited the Oberhaus Museum and saw the "Jewish cellars," where Jews had been tortured during the Middle Ages. Some of the instruments of torture were displayed as part of the exhibit.

My father was right: this time I really didn't know *anything*. Despite my "A" in history! But something more important happened: my ambition was awakened. I realized I had to shed this stigma of ignorance.

My father could not help me out with ideas on this topic. He was a "displaced person,"—whatever that was. In any case, he had not been living in Passau during the time in question. My mother had been too young. She was three years old when Hitler assumed power. When Hitler started the war she had just turned ten. If anyone were to ask me about events that occurred when I was three, four, five, or even ten years old, I could not have given them any answers either.

My grandmother, who was eighty-three at the time, told me that she was too old to remember exactly what had happened. She had lost her husband before the war and had had terrible financial troubles. More than once she had stood in front of the gas stove in her kitchen, wondering whether she shouldn't stick her head in it and turn up the gas, as so many others were doing at the time. She had had no place in her life for political antics and intrigues. She had had to fight for her and her family's survival. "Most likely," she said "there was nothing special happening in Passau during that time; after all, it was so small and so far away from everything." My uncle told me that he had just started school in those days, and that later, when he was studying for the priesthood, he was living at the seminary and leading a life that was secluded from the outside world.

Wouldn't that be something, I thought, if nobody could tell me anything? My uncle suggested I get in touch with Dr. Emil Janik. He was the editor in chief of the weekly newsletter of the diocese of Passau, the *Passauer Bistumsblatt*, from the years before the war up until then. He had to know what had taken place. In addition, he recommended I visit the state archives and the Episcopal Archives. That's where the files would be. I should also talk with an old friend of his, Dr. Schäffer, who was very familiar with the local heritage and, at the very least, could point me in the direction of what I was looking for. My uncle also suggested asking Dr. Lampert, who was rumored to have helped organize armed local resistance to the Nazis. And then there was Dr. Enthofer, the man who had been in charge of the local seminary; he suggested I be careful in dealing him, though; even as little boys they were always careful when they were around him. And if he was not willing to talk, there was Dr. Gantenberg in Büchlberg: he was a real fighter back then and got into all kinds of trouble with the Nazi regime. And, of course, there was the Bishop himself, Dr. Antonius Hofmann. He was about the right age to know a few things on the subject.

My uncle was a geyser of knowledge; one slight jostle and before you knew it, everything just came spewing out of him. What seemed logical to him, however, was not so easy for me to understand. For example, up until then I didn't even know that we had such a thing as archives, not to mention where they were located or what could be done with them. Of all the names my uncle had mentioned I knew only one of them, and not very well at that: Bishop Hofmann. He had confirmed me into the Church and paid the occasional visit to my uncle and my grandmother. I noted down the other names, looked up their phone numbers, and began to ask questions.

At that point my research was not yet very specific, my direction not yet defined. At the same time, however, I was certain that the Catholic Church, all-powerful as it was in Passau, would be a good source for noteworthy material. I was searching for photographs; I asked about people who had been part of the resistance. I didn't get very far: Dr. Schäffer reportedly knew nothing. Dr. Lampert died a few days after I had called him. Dr. Janik at first refused to say anything and then, a short time later, also died. Dr. Enthofer claimed to have made a vow never to speak about the issue again (Irritated, I asked my mother what a "vow" (*Eid*) was). Bishop Hofmann initially was away taking the cure (*zur Kur*) in a sanitarium; after his return he refused to tell me anything and sent me home—"And be sure to tell your uncle that I send my greetings" were his last words to me. In the city archives I was presented with stacks of huge folios, each of which listed innumerable old folders. Strangely enough all the controversial ones had been "lost"—at least that's what I was told. At the Episcopal Archives I was refused access to the files. The reasons I was given were different every time, each more ludicrous that the last.

I was beginning to wonder about these strange coincidences. My ignorance about the subject I was researching was not exactly something to be proud of. That my closest relatives knew nothing was regrettable. But was it possible that no one else knew anything, either? I was getting annoyed about how long everything was taking—my last essay was researched, written, and delivered in less time!

I also found it odd that people were being so unfriendly and dismissive. They were not apologetic in the least if they didn't know anything. I went to the *Passauer Bistumsblatt* and asked to see the old archived editions. Else Janik was working there; she was a sister of Dr. Emil Janik and of Agathe Janik, who had been my first teacher. I had always liked her and she me. When I was a little girl she used to give me the keys to her house so I could water her plants while she was away on vacation. In exchange she brought me back shells from the beach, which I kept for many years. I always sat in the front row in her class. When I was sick—and that was a lot during elementary school—Agathe Janik would call my mother and ask her when I would be coming back because she could not teach without me. Agathe had been the first person to congratulate me on my engagement and the first one to bring a wedding gift to the house before my wedding. Another of Agathe's brothers, Rudolf, had once offered to adopt my mother if my grandmother were to die unexpectedly. Once, as a result of being overworked during the war, my grandmother had developed and nearly died from a thyroid poisoning. When, as a result, my mother was temporarily sent to the orphanage, her chaplain, Rudolf Janik, offered to take care of her instead.

My search had led me to Agathe and Rudolf's sister, Else. Else Janik's reaction to my request was initially brusque. Suspicious, she asked me again for my name. When I told her, she apologized and told me that, of course I could read them. I could even take them home with me over the weekend if I wanted. Else was the first person to help me. Once at home I began searching for useful material. Much of it was quite fascinating and I became transfixed by what I read. The paper I was reading was dated 1936, the first year of publication. But there was nothing at all about resistance in what I read. On the contrary, the articles I found by Dr. Emil Janik made my hair stand on end: "Let's pray for the *Führer* and our Fatherland!" There was an enthusiastic article offering congratulations on "the *Führer's*" birthday—and there was the following justification for the war of aggression, written by Janik, which appeared in the *Bistumsblatt:*

"Our People: Fighting for *Lebensraum*"

After God had created the world he instructed man to "be fruitful, and multiply, and replenish the earth, and subdue it!" And man obeyed and so from the very beginning started his search for space to live. When the first communities formed, the problem of space became more complex. Eventually there emerged new peoples and nations who were conscious of the *Lebensraum* they required. Thereafter, nations developed that began to divide up the world according to their own needs, claiming for themselves a disproportionately large share of the world and thereby putting others, who owing to their productivity and population desperately needed larger territories for their expansion, at a disadvantage. Certainly, this unjust distribution of space goes against God's will. We Germans cannot help but wonder: why is England allowed to rule two-thirds of the world while Germany, which is much larger, is squeezed into such a small space on a crowded European continent, and what is more, is not even allowed to administer the colonies it so honestly acquired? Why? Because the very legitimate claim of our German nation to a sufficiently large *Lebensraum* has not been granted. That it is why Germany is at war today. The *Lebensraum* on earth, if justly distributed amongst the nations according to their size and importance, is large and ample and bountiful enough to afford all nations a peaceful and harmonious existence, as it is in God's plan. Unfortunately, the wealthy and powerful nations of the world have not yet realized this. Once obtained, they want to hold on to their sphere of influence at all cost, even if populous and aspiring nations such as Germany live in dire need of space. From this vantage point the present war can be explained in very simple terms: *today our German nation is fighting for its growth and its Lebensraum.* It is not Germany's aim to suppress other peoples or to conquer other countries; instead, we fight for the same rights and the same claims to earth's rich bounty already granted to all other peoples. This struggle for our God-given rights instills in every German, whether at the front or at home, the will to persevere with great strength, until justice reigns victorious in the world.

I was speechless. I knew little about Emil Janik and less about National Socialism, but it was clear that *this* could not in any way be called resistance. I took the articles home to show them to my parents and asked them what they thought about them, how they could explain them. My father didn't find them as horrific as I did; he told me that this was simply the way it was (*Zeitgeist*) in those days, but he had to admit that it certainly could not pass for resistance. Maybe Dr. Janik had been blackmailed into writing such an article, or maybe somebody else had attributed the article to him without his knowledge or consent? Back then all kinds of things were going on with the Church, things that were difficult to imagine today. He suggested, as did my mother, that I give Dr. Janik another call. After all, this time I was not asking questions about the Nazi period in general, but about his personal conduct and about concrete newspaper articles; certainly he would be prepared to talk about that.

I took my parents' advice and called him back. I briefly told him how perplexed I was and asked if, at any point back then, he had been blackmailed, or whether any texts had been forged or if perhaps somebody had falsely attributed a newspaper article to him. . . ? Dr. Janik's reaction was curt, but very clear: quite the opposite was true, he said. He himself had written the articles just as they appeared. He had not been blackmailed and he had signed his name to them voluntarily. Others had not been able to identify with his articles and that's why he had signed his name, in order to show that this was his opinion. I was stunned—I had not expected so much frankness, nor was I prepared for this kind of admission. I took the opportunity to ask him about the strange anti-Jewish articles that had been published in the *Bistumsblatt*. Had they been forced onto the paper by the Nazi regime? With astonishing honesty Dr. Janik replied: "No, back then we were against the Jews. That's how we grew up; we had learned to despise the Jews; to us they represented evil itself—just like the Communists more recently. Nobody had to force us; that's how it was back then and I wrote what I thought. It's not as though *everything* back then was wrong."

Not only could I not accept his opinion, I could not understand it, and I would never approve of it. But I had to admit I was impressed by his openness. He was neither rude nor did he try to be evasive. He spoke without pause. I asked him whether I could quote him directly on his ideas, and he told me, "But of course." I thanked him and jotted down my notes. My father copied the articles in question for me and I returned the volumes to the library on Monday. I tried to understand how a person could "despise" Jews. I didn't know any Jews and knew absolutely nothing about Judaism, but I knew that Jesus had been a Jew, as had been his mother. . . . If we Catholics were praying to Jesus as the Son of God and were worshiping his mother, how, then, could Catholics be against the Jews? Up until then I hadn't heard anything about anti-Semitism or about the racial fanaticism of the Nazis.

Just as I had done all my life when I was worried, I went to see my mother—who was living in the house next door to us. I asked if back then she, too, had been against the Jews, and what Emil Janik could have meant when he said, "That's just how we were back then." She told me about her religious instruction in school back then. She told me how, for instance, they were told to pray "for the Jewish unbelievers" on each Good Friday; this practice had remained part of the Good Friday litany until just a few years ago. Back then, most pupils found the caricatures of Jews funny. She herself had not known any Jews, but her mother, my Granny, sometimes shopped at a Jewish store. The owner's name was Klein and he sold ready-to-wear men's clothes. Her brothers' suits came from there and they were especially durable. She did not know what ultimately happened to the store.

But then she began to remember a few specific incidents, and they got my attention. They were scenes from her daily school life: as a little girl she wrote excellent essays and one time she won first prize in a writing competition. Her reward was a book titled *Poodle-Pug-Dachshund-Pinscher*. She was happy because naturally she thought it was a book about dogs. She was very disappointed to find out that it was not about dogs, but contained strange and distorted images—caricatures of Jews. She then recalled how it was said back then that Jews had crooked legs, like dachshunds, and ugly, scrunched little faces, like pugs . . . She didn't like the book and didn't keep it.

There was another time, when my mother was in eighth grade, that her teacher, Ms. Hausner, said to her, "Annerl, what do you say we both have our names changed when the war is over." Both of their first names were Anna, and back then this was considered "too Jewish."

Then she told me about Ms. Hartl, who was always sitting in the very back of her store. "She was a big, quiet woman," she said. "She may have been Jewish. Her daughter's name was Uschi, and later her last name was Eichberger. She might have more to tell you."

This is all my mother could remember regarding Jews "back then."

My curiosity continued to grow; my name was Anna as well—after my grandmother. What did that mean—Jewish? My uncle told me that back then at "his" high school (which I had of course attended as well) the teacher had told them every morning before classes: "The Jews are our misfortune!" And this at a "humanistic" high school! Nobody had ever told us anything about Jews, but we had always been admonished to respect others in principle, and not to discriminate against anyone because of his skin color or his religion. I was bewildered.

My grandmother acknowledged that, yes, sometimes she had shopped at the "Kleins." The store was called "Klein Brothers" and, yes, the owner had been Jewish. That's why they were told not to shop there. "A lot of rubbish, that." she said. "The quality there was very good and prices weren't high; where else should we have shopped?" She continued: "There was another Jew, just across the street," in what is now the city's pedestrian zone. Their last name was Pick. They also had excellent goods and they always had good deals. But my Granny could not remember what had happened to them. "The stores remained open," she recalls, "but then they had different names." "Klein" was renamed "Hofmax" . . . No! she suddenly remembered. His son-in-law, Zacharias, had taken it over. The store still exists today. No, he wasn't a Jew, my grandmother recalled. What she did not realize was that the shop had been "Aryanized," that Nathan Klein had been forced to give up the business after he had been blackmailed by one of his former apprentices.

Six weeks had gone by and I wasn't even close to having collected enough material to write my essay. And it didn't look as though that would change any time soon.

I wanted to know and find out about what the real issue was with these Jews. I wanted to know where the rage against them came from, and what had finally happened to them. Because nobody could or would give me a straight answer I went to the national library and asked for more old newspapers. I was given one volume after another, with no questions asked. I started reading, beginning with the year 1933, about the "Prewar Years in my Hometown."

I didn't have far to look before I found what I was looking for. Nathan Klein and Julius Pick had run advertisements in the paper; another "special insert" (*Sonderseite*) introduced the concentration camp Dachau, which had "finally" been completed . . . I was completely stunned and reeling from the shock. I spent days and weeks in the library, reading newspapers. The scales fell from my eyes. It suddenly became clear to me, the reasons why nobody had wanted to talk to me, why no one was prepared to answer my questions!

The more I read the more gruesome the facts became. And we had never been told a single thing about this! I was twenty years old, I had lived in this town for twenty years, and I had not the slightest knowledge of any of this. How could it be that none of it was ever mentioned in social studies class at school? How was it that we had studied in detail and even come to understand so much about the cultures of ancient Egypt and Rome, and knew nothing about what had happened right outside our front doors? We had studied the Punic Wars and all kinds of battles dating back to antiquity—yet knew nothing about the madness of Hitler?

I remembered that one of the teachers had briefly addressed the Second World War in our final year of high school. At the beginning of the lesson he had hung a huge map on the board and pointed out various cities: on this and that day/month/year this and that treaty was signed in this and that city. Thereafter the border had "moved" from here to there. On this and that day/month/year this treaty was signed in that city . . . The border then "moved" again.

I had been listening to his lecture for some time and remember thinking that it sounded as if he were reading directly from tables and charts; he recited lists of dates and names without rhyme or reason, and continued reciting, with no end in sight. I raised my hand and politely asked what he meant, exactly, when he said the border had "moved"; borders don't just "move," I said. And certainly it couldn't be so easy to just move them. I wanted to know *who* moved them and *why* it had happened. . . . The teacher simply continued reciting his dates, as if I had never spoken. I became angry and demanded—in a loud voice and without first being called on—that he explain to us the historical background and the reasons for these events; after all, if all we wanted was a list of dates and names, we could look them up for ourselves. Our teacher became quite irritated; his voice grew very quiet and began to tremble as he continued quoting dates and names to us. I'd had it! I didn't want to spoil the class with a fight; after all, I had been the only person complaining. But I wanted him to know how much I resented what he was doing. So I quietly I turned my chair around and sat facing the wall. The teacher was beside himself. Snorting with rage, he left the classroom and returned only at the end of the session.

That was the extent, I suppose, of our lesson on National Socialism.

This event did have a sequel, however: our teacher happened to run into my mother on the street one day, while she was shopping. He told her how I had turned around my chair in protest and how he was unable to go on teaching after that. What kind of behavior was that? he asked. And I had not even bothered to apologize! Of course I had already told her all about the incident. A few months later we were preparing to take an important test (the grade would show up on our final transcript). We were asked to learn, by heart, among other things all the dates he had mentioned in that lecture. I stared at him and asked if he was serious. Cynically he replied, "Yes. And even *you* will study for this one, Miss Rosmus. After all, the grade is very important here!" "What a pig!" I thought, and I promised myself not to study the dates—not unless he explained something about their context. "We'll see about that next week," he remarked smugly. The following week was test week. Our teacher seated me—just this once—directly in front of his desk, the idea being, I suppose, that there I wouldn't be able to cheat. I obediently walked to the front, sat down, and began writing under his watchful eye.

He had a big grin on his face when he returned my exam a short time later. All of the dates and names I had written down were correct and complete. "So you did study, after all," he commented.

He was wrong.

We both had earned our small victory, each in his own way.

Much more important than either "victory," however, was the fact that we had graduated knowing nothing about the context, about the reasons behind the genocide committed against Jews, Sinti and Roma gypsies, about the massacres, and the suffering of the victims. Given the chance, I would have all too willingly pored over the history books, even back then, in order to learn the truth about what happened.

Almost a year passed. I sat and read, and I asked people who had lived during those times for their interpretations. I typed throughout the

Christmas holidays. I pieced things together as best I could. I quoted from the old newspapers, which boasted shamelessly about how "brown" (as in full of brownshirts) a city Passau was back then. In the end I even succeeded in digging up a few photographs. Classes were starting back, and so I went back to the university . . . and typed late into the night to make sure that I would make the contest deadline of January 31st, 1981.

Right up to the last minute Dr. Wurster, the archivist of the Diocesan Archives, kept up his delaying tactics, giving me many different reasons why I could not use its records. Each one more absurd than the last. At the end of January, I made one last attempt to get my hands on at least a few of the documents: the death sentences of the Catholic priests Mitterer and Winkler, whose murders had been politically motivated. Again, my request was denied. My mother told Dr. Wurster that she found this all very strange: almost nothing was known about these two martyrs, and now that somebody wanted to write about them, the Church, of all things, was preventing it. Dr. Wurster explained to her, that it was simply not worth all the trouble it would take for a simple "class project"; he would have to search for the materials and that could take a very long time. But, he added, if I intended to perhaps write a book one day, then of course I would be given access to the files.

By this time I had become suspicious; he had broken his promises to me too many times and I did not trust him any more. Still, to make sure I was not being unfair I decided to get some proof. At home I picked up the telephone book, turned to the yellow pages, and started looking up publishing houses. I called the first one I found and asked if they would be interested in a book dealing with the prewar years in Passau, as I was writing a paper on this subject at present for an essay competition. The publisher remembered right away that I had received a prize for my last essay, and he told me he could imagine that there would be a good deal of popular interest in such a project, since nothing had yet been written on the topic. He offered right then and there to print the manuscript as soon as it was completed. It ought to be published as soon as possible, he said.

I could not believe my ears: he didn't even need to see the manuscript. But because I now wanted to take Dr. Wurster up on his "offer," I asked the publisher to give me his offer in writing.

I only had a few hours left until the deadline, and was typing like a maniac to finish the final pages. But I still didn't have an introduction. Instead of including a regular introduction, I made a detailed list of when, where, and by whom my research had been obstructed, who had provided me with materials and who had denied me access, where I eventually was able to get information and who—intentionally or not—had misled me. At four-thirty in the morning I was done. At eight A.M. I started making copies. There were about 260 pages and I had to duplicate each page separately—we didn't have faster copy machines in Passau in those days. Exhausted, I asked my mother to come get me and drive me to the main post office. The letter had to be postmarked with that day's date. The clerk was just about to close up when we arrived. I still had to address the letter, I still needed stamps—and I wanted to send it by registered mail. Shaking his head, the clerk handed me the stamps and my receipt for the registered letter and closed up behind us.

Totally exhausted, I slept for nearly two days. A short time later the mailman delivered the letter I had been waiting for: the publishing house was going to publish my manuscript! My spirits were immediately lifted. The first thing I did was to go back to Dr. Wurster and tell him that I would indeed be writing a book. The subject would be "Resistance and Persecution in Passau, 1933–1939." As I spoke the words, I could barely suppress the cynicism in my voice.

Dr. Wurster stared at me silently, and handed me another official request form, which consisted of multiple pages. I obediently filled it out for the second time: name, topic of research. I would be notified in a few days, he told me—just like he had told me the last time.

My mother had accompanied me to the Episcopal Archives, so that I would have a witness. And again I got the run-around, this time because he had not expected me to be writing a book so soon. I would have to come back later, I was told, once I had officially received my master's degree.

I was more annoyed than disappointed. My suspicions had just been confirmed. I crossed Dr. Wurster and his archives off my list—at least for the time being.

I finished my first semester at the university, but then became pregnant and, due to almost constant morning sickness, stayed at home a few times during my second semester. Because I had been absent more than three times I wasn't allowed to take the written exams and didn't get credit for my courses. I decided to take a leave of absence and just like that became a "simple housewife."

In the fall of 1981 there was still no news about the results of the essay competition: approximately 13,000 students had submitted papers for the last competition of the Körber Foundation in Hamburg. The jury was swamped with papers. Finally, in the spring of 1982, the winners had been

determined: I won third place. The jury commended me on having succeeded in drawing such a clear picture of the time in spite of the numerous obstacles I had to overcome.

The competition itself had been around for a long time, but never
before had a topic motivated so many students to participate and never
before had a subject excited the public as much as this one had. The official patron of the competition was the then president of the Federal
Republic of Germany (*Bundespräsident*), Dr. Carl Carstens. He himself
had been a member of the "stormtroopers," or Sturmabteilung (SA), back
then, and for this reason many people believed he shouldn't have been
allowed to be a part of "this kind of thing." Others admired him precisely
because he had taken part anyway. Dieter Galinski, the manager of the
foundation, informed the winners later on that the *Bundespräsident* had
actually signed the call for papers before the topic had even been determined.

Due to the unusually high number of submissions, the excellent quality
of the work, and the great public interest, the Friedrich-Ebert-Foundation,
named after the German socialist leader and president of the post-World
War I Weimar Republic, decided to invite some of the prize winners to a
seminar in Bonn. We were to have a chance to meet politicians, historians,
and journalists and to talk about our research experiences. Among those
invited was Michael Brenner, a Jewish man from Weiden, who had written about his own family. His contribution was later published as a book
for adolescents by the Fischer publishing house. Ten years after the competition I had a chance to talk to him again: I was presenting "my" film
in New York; he was writing his dissertation there—after finishing his
degree in Israel. Another prizewinner who had been invited was Jens
Rehländer, who also later went to New York; he had received a scholar-
ship from the Körber Foundation to live among homeless people for a few
weeks and to write a report about his experiences. As a result of his project he was later hired as an editor for the Hamburg popular science magazine *GEO*. One of our conversation partners was former chancellor Willy
Brandt, who had gone into exile during the Nazi era and had been active
in the resistance. Another was Josef Felder, the last surviving member
of the former *Reichstag* delegates who back then had voted against the
"Enabling Act," a bill that would have given Hitler's government dictato-
rial powers. Josef Felder made a special impression on me: I liked the
openness with which he spoke and listened to us young people.

When I told him about the problems I was having with some of the archives and mentioned that I had already been threatened with various lawsuits he asked me whether I had insurance to cover potential legal costs—just in case. During the break he gave me the address of Martin Hirsch in Karlsruhe and suggested that I get in touch with him, because, he said, "he knows all about that kind of thing."

Chapter 3

THE JUDGE AT THE FEDERAL CONSTITUTIONAL COURT

I HAD NEVER HEARD of Martin Hirsch. I thanked Mr. Felder for the address anyway. It couldn't hurt to give him a call. Give Hirsch my regards, Mr. Felder added. The break was over. I answered a few more of the journalists' questions and left.

Back in Passau I continued to search through old newspapers. I also wrote to Mr. Hirsch. I assumed he knew all the ins and outs of legal costs insurance, and so I asked his advice about protecting myself from the lawsuits I might face. A few days later I received an answer. The return address on the letterhead read: *Martin Hirsch, ret. Judge of the Federal Constitutional Court*. I couldn't believe my eyes. I kept reading it over and over again as if it couldn't possibly be true. I tore open the envelope and what I found was one of the kindest letters ever written to me: he was not an expert on the topic of legal costs insurance, but he would be happy to assist me in any way he could. It would be best, he said, if I would simply pack up the manuscript and come to see him in Karlsruhe. He would look through it with me and then tell me what I should do.

He said that he lived in a high-rise apartment building and that I could stay with him. A female colleague of his lived in the same building, and if I preferred I could stay at her place. I only needed to let him know which train I would be taking and he would pick me up himself at the station. He told me he would be driving a white sports car, wearing a white baseball cap, and holding a copy of the Frankfurt newspaper, the *Frankfurter Allgemeine Zeitung* (*FAZ*) so that I would recognize him. My husband flew into a rage and belittled me for my naivety: didn't I know what it meant when a man "invites" a young woman to spend the night at his place? Feeling dazed I went next door to my parents' house and asked them if the letter could be for real. My father calmly read the letter and told me that yes, indeed, he knew of Martin Hirsch. And my uncle, who was visiting, knew right off the bat that he was an member of the liberal Social Democratic Party (SPD). My mother didn't say anything at first. After a few seconds of general silence, she told me to go ahead and go. "Just be careful," she said.

Careful was exactly what I intended to be: the thrill of the new, the unknown, was tempting me again. Of course I didn't know exactly what I was getting myself into. I wasn't even sure if my husband wasn't perhaps right after all. But I had always been the curious type, and it was hard to resist such an unconventional invitation. Besides, he might really be able to help me. I didn't know who else to turn to. I completed the manuscript as fast as I could and wrote to Mr. Hirsch to tell him which train I would be taking. I packed a few essentials and was on my way.

When I arrived at the train station in Karlsruhe, there were lots of people standing around, but no one wearing a baseball cap and carrying the *FAZ*. As I made my way to the exit, a portly, older gentleman with glasses and white hair was coming toward me. He grinned and greeted me. It was Martin Hirsch. Grandfatherly type, I thought, relieved.

Mr. Hirsch showed me around Karlsruhe. We first visited the Constitutional Court, where he had been judge until very recently. He showed me the law offices where he now worked, and then we went to his house. "A typical terrorist's house," he joked, "with two exits!" He showed me my room and I set down my luggage. Then he took me to meet his colleague, Diemut Majer. She was a lawyer and the first German academic allowed to freely conduct research in the Polish archives. Her book *Rassefremde in Deutschland* (*Racial Aliens in Germany*) had received major international attention. Her specialty was administrative law, and later she would become instrumental in helping me to successfully bring a lawsuit against the City of Passau. But back then I couldn't have predicted any of this.

That evening Mr. Hirsch took both of us out to a gourmet restaurant. I told him about Passau, about my work, and about the threats that had been raining down on me like stones for quite some time now. He did not seem surprised. Diemut Majer told me about the difficulties she found herself in after she had published the legal drafts in which the Nazis had clearly stated just how ruthlessly they would be dealing with their remaining enemies once the "final victory" was secured. Mr. Hirsch told us stories about how, during his tenure on the Federal Constitutional Court, he had earned the reputation of being a maverick through his "deviationist opinions." But that was nothing new for him. During the Nazi era most of his colleagues had joined the Party in order not to ruin their career chances. He had refused to do so, however, and he ultimately paid for it heavily. When he was drafted into the army he made it a point not to be promoted beyond the lowest rank.

He said that he had come to appreciate the courage it took to make a stand against those things that, though accepted by a majority, are nonetheless offensive. That was why he continued to support young people who were standing up for what they believed in. He asked me if I had heard of Brigitte Schanderl from Regensburg; she had gotten into serious trouble because she had worn a "Stop Strauss" pin to school in protest of the ultra-conservative politician's bid to become *Bundeskanzler*. He had defended her, because, after all, her right to free speech was guaranteed in the constitution, was it not?

I was not familiar with the case, even though Regensburg and Passau are only sixty miles apart. He stayed up half the night reading my manuscript and the next morning told me how good it was. He promised to write the preface and to come to Passau, where he insisted that the book should be publicly released. He suggested we use the *Scharfrichterhaus* (Executioners' House) for the event. It would be the perfect place to attract the attention of the press, and an official visit from a Constitutional Court Judge to Passau would be impossible to keep under wraps. He would use his name, his title, and his respectability to support my project; that would be better than any insurance. I liked the idea and I liked Martin Hirsch's sense of adventure. That evening, the three of us went to a huge party, organized by the SPD, in honor of his seventieth birthday. I could barely wait for the event in Passau.

Chapter 4

FIFTY YEARS AFTER THE
SEIZURE OF POWER

THE FIFTIETH ANNIVERSARY of Hitler's seizure of power was approaching. The City of Passau would be recognizing the occasion. This time an official commemoration, commonplace in most other German cities, was planned for the first time since the Second World War. Discussions about who should speak, how to commemorate the occasion, and where to hold the events were taking place everywhere, be it at the *Scharfrichterhaus* or the Catholic Community Educational Program or the Community Youth Group. I was invited to all of them; I was the only one who had researched the subject and received a prize for my work. I readily agreed to lead a weekend event for Catholic adolescents at the Oberhaus Castle, even though I had never done anything like it before. I immediately agreed when a Marist monk asked me to visit his school and give a presentation to the upper grades. I also agreed when the Community Youth Group asked me to introduce my book at an event to be held at the university. I hesitated, however, when Edgar Liegl from the *Scharfrichterhaus* called me. They were planning a "homeland program" (*Heimatabend*) featuring Passau's best known political satirists (*Kabarettisten*), a few musicians—and me.

I was stunned: the *Scharfrichterhaus*? It was right down the street from my high school. Some of the students used to hang out there when they would cut classes. Some of them would meet there in the evenings to listen to jazz or to see the cabaret. Political cabaret, of course. Siegfried Zimmerschied, Passau's bad boy number one back then, had had his first performances there—and as a result was showered with the collective hatred of the City and the Catholic Church. He had been flooded with lawsuits because in his skit "Conference in Heaven," he had, among other things, spoken about Mary's second pregnancy, for which the Holy Ghost had refused to acknowledge paternity. He ultimately won his case. "Artistic freedom" was the judge's magic word. Zimmerschied and I had attended the same school. He was a couple of years older than me. Bruno Jonas, a well-known television comedian and satirist, had also gotten his start at the Executioner's House. He had attended my school and graduated just a few years before me. And then there was Rudi Klaffenböck with his "reality satires" (*Realsatiren*). He, too, had attended the *Leopoldinum*. We all came from the same strict Catholic background. And we'd all had similar experiences with our hometown. But they had become satirists and remained unconventional, on the fringe. I, however, was without question still a member of the establishment. I would never have been allowed to go to the *Scharfrichterhaus*. I wouldn't even have dared to ask my parents' permission to go there. The *Scharfrichterhaus* was completely taboo—a "den of iniquity" (*Sündenpfuhl*), it was called. I myself had never been there, even though it is located right next to City Hall. And now I was talking on the phone with Edgar Liegl, as if it were the most natural thing in the world. I was speechless. There he was, telling me what he wanted me to do: I should just get up and talk for five minutes or so—no more—about the seizure of power in Passau. Just the facts about what had happened back then. Assuming I knew something about the topic.

You will be coming, won't you? he asked finally.

Yes, I said. I would. No further explanations.

Mr. Liegl didn't seem surprised. He simply hung up, satisfied. I tried to sum up the situation in my head, to no avail, so I simply shook my head in dismay and left. I couldn't stop thinking about what had just happened. What would my parents say if I were to appear at the *Scharfrichterhaus*? I went next door to see my mother and told her where I my next speaking engagement would be. I had by then come up with my explanation for the situation: it didn't make any difference whether I talked about this topic at the Marist Cloister or at the *Scharfrichterhaus*. After all, facts are facts.

My mother stared at me silently.

I guess it did make a difference, after all. She didn't prevent me from going there though. Initially that fact managed to calm my fears somewhat. A few days later large, bright red posters were posted on every street corner in Passau: the *Scharfrichterhaus* had announced its schedule for the month of January. There, printed next to the names of the political satirists, was my name.

But before the *Heimatabend* took place, an event at the university was scheduled. Dr. Hermann Gantenberg and I were scheduled to speak. Dr. Gantenberg was one of those rare Catholic clergymen who had been part of the resistance and who had suffered for it. He was a man who had been more or less forgotten by the public. At the beginning of my research my uncle had told me about him. I had visited him several times and received valuable material from him. I dedicated an entire chapter to him and in this way helped him gain a sort of belated fame. His community quickly named a street after him and made him an honorable citizen of the city (*hat ihm die Ehrenbürgerwürde verliehen*). And now he was set to speak on the subject of "Resistance and Persecution in Passau." But it never came to be. Shortly before the event he suddenly fell very ill and had to cancel on short notice. I was on my own.

The Community Youth Center had arranged to rent the large auditorium. It held four hundred people and was nearly filled to capacity when I arrived. As I approached the stage an older gentleman asked me if I had already brought a glass of water for the speaker. Slightly amused, I told him that the speaker would not need one, and walked up to the podium. The man stared at me as if he'd seen a ghost. Later he apologized; I looked so young, he said, that he hadn't expected that. I'm sure he meant it as a compliment, as he then added: "But you spoke like an old pro!" Judging by the applause, there were many others who also had thought so, too.

The discussion that followed was lively. The audience's curiosity was great—and their knowledge of the subject apparently poor. Some of the questions were extremely awkward. A former fellow student from my German class who was now working as a journalist for the *Passau Daily News* (*Passauer Neue Presse*, *PNP*) wanted to know whether Emil Janik "had really been as 'brown' as people say," or if these claims were exaggerated. Janik had been the editor in chief of the *Passauer Bistumsblatt* before, during, and after the war, without any interruption, until the day he died. His brother Erwin was editor in chief of the *PNP*. He lived right down the street from me. His wife was a teacher, a colleague of my parents; my parents had been guests in the Janik household before. The "official" story was that his brother Emil had been a resistance fighter. And now this question!

I answered as clearly and completely as I could: in my opinion he had neither been "brown" in the literal sense of being an active member of the "brownshirts," nor had he been a resistance fighter. I quoted from some of his articles: they were quite horrifying. I talked about the fact that it must have indeed been very difficult for him back then. It certainly wasn't easy, as a Catholic priest, to write damning articles about the Nazi regime. In essence I had defended him, with a few obvious exceptions.

Some people hissed (*pfiffen*) and some shouted that I was defending him too much, but they quickly calmed down again and more questions were asked. I answered patiently; only once, I would later learn, did I (unknowingly) provide them with false information: Johann Fröhler asked about the three concentration camps in Passau, if I knew anything about them. I had never heard or read anything about this and I simply could not imagine that there were ever any concentration camps in Passau. I told him: "No," and that he must be mistaken about that.

Everybody seemed satisfied.

Chapter 5

THE JANIK TRIAL

ON THE MORNING AFTER the event I ran into my former Latin teacher in town. He asked me how I was and I told him casually: "Fine, thank you." Then he leaned over and whispered to me in a strangely secretive voice: "Why do you have to go and open your mouth? You'll just get in trouble. I know more than you think." This was very atypical behavior for him. He had been the one who suggested that I attend the *Leopoldinum*, back in 1976. He had always been there for me; sometimes it seemed he knew me better than I knew myself. He had remained by my side through-out the years, as student counselor and as a friend. I could always go to see him, and I had often done so. Lots of us had. For years the two of us had celebrated birthdays together. We had even gone out together; just before my oral examination he had waited for me in the hallway and offered me a piece of marzipan to calm my nerves. Before my wedding he had gone up to *Mariahilf*, our local pilgrimage church and monastery perched on a hill high above the city, to pray for me. He had come to my wedding. . . . So I truly did not understand his remark. Even his tone was strange, unfamiliar. Before I had a chance to ask him what he meant he had already walked off.

That evening I received a call from Erwin Janik. He asked me if I knew why he was calling? How could I agree to speak to the public at the *Scharfrichterhaus?* he scolded: He had seen the posters hanging all over town. A short while later an editor from the *PNP* phoned: he had just been asked to sign a deposition in a court case brought against me, and asked for my understanding. He had signed. He didn't want me to think that he had anything against me, but he was afraid of losing his job. Of course he knew that it hadn't been my intention to. . . . I had no idea what this man was talking about! I had known him for years. His son had gone to school with my brother and used to play ping-pong at our house. He himself had waited outside the *Leopoldinum* more than once offering to drive me home.

He lived in our neighborhood. I didn't trust him, though, and so had never taken him up on it. I also frequently ran into him at dances, where I went to try to avoid him. What was he calling me about? He explained to me that it had to do with Janik, and with what I had said about him at the university. One of my mother's colleagues, Anni Lang, had been in the audience, and she had told Erwin Janik what I had said. Her version was slightly different from what had actually happened, and he had been asked to officially confirm this version in a written and signed declaration. He assured me that I could still call him any time if I needed anything, but in this case he had decided to sign.

I thought all this very strange. I had seen Anni Lang that night, but why had Janik, and not she, called me? What exactly could he have signed? I had, after all, defended Janik's brother, in spite of the jeers and hisses it had I'd gotten for it. I continued preparing for my appearance at the *Scharfrichterhaus*, which was now only a few hours away.

When I arrived I didn't recognize anyone. My disoriented look gave me away, and Edgar Liegl recognized me. He approached me and asked how I was, and I briefly told him and the others about the strange phone calls I'd received. Just then the telephone in the *Scharfrichterhaus* rang again. It was my husband. He was still at home and had just been presented with an injunction against me. The bailiff had delivered it in person. He hadn't had to go very far to deliver it, since he too lived in the neighborhood, between Erwin Janik's house and ours. My husband didn't know him and had no idea what to do with the document. Nor did I, and so I asked Mr. Liegl what we should do.

Unlike me, the "*Scharfrichter* crowd" had extensive experience dealing with such injunctions—especially ones originating from Erwin Janik. They asked if they could have a look at the document. I asked my husband if he could bring it by. Fifteen minutes later we were holding it in our hands. The district court officially forbade me to repeat tonight what I had said about Emil Janik at the university; I had never had any intention of doing so, nor had I given any indication that I had planned to do such a thing. Rudolf Klaffenböck, Bruno Jonas, and Siegfried Zimmerschied disappeared with the document into an adjacent room. They promised me they'd come up with something; I didn't have a clue what that might be. In the meantime the hall was bursting with people. Anni Lang was sitting in the first row, with her daughters. Further back sat the editor. Liegl had wanted to keep him off the premises because of his story with the signed declaration, but I had asked him to be lenient. After all, I said, he had "confessed," and I did not want anybody to lose his job. But I did tell him that I would see him in court, where he would have to explain to a jury why he had signed his name to such false allegations. The lights dimmed and the performance began. A visitor from Munich was recording everything on videotape. The performers had come up with a witty, light hearted but acerbic skit dealing with the injunction. The audience went wild. It was not entirely clear to us whether they realized that only the act was cabaret, but that the incident itself was all too real.

Afterwards one of the Passau *Kabarettisten* read out the preliminary injunction to the audience and pointed out that this was not cabaret, this was reality. The crowd applauded enthusiastically. "That Janik, he never learns," some people whispered, but most of the comments were about how perfect, how convincing the political satire was. The *Kabarettist* stepped down from the stage and made his way through the rows of people, letting them see the official document for themselves, confirming that it was real and that it had been sent to me by the bailiff less than an hour ago. The applause and laughter increased even more. Obviously nobody quite believed it. The program continued: theater, music—and finally me, with my five-minute factual report on the "Nazi Seizure of Power in Passau."

My heart was racing when I stepped onto the stage; I saw Anni Lang and her daughters right in front of me. I couldn't help but open my speech with a slight jab at her: "Dear listeners and eavesdroppers," I began. Then I proceeded to report very factually about how the election results of our home town had been manipulated back then, how quickly the banners with the swastikas had been raised atop City Hall and the Catholic University, and how, in honor of Hitler, an oak tree had been planted at the confluence of the three rivers on the edge of town. I mentioned the fact that, according to press information back then, dogs used to do their business right by the tree, and so some SA men had been assigned to guard the "memorial" day and night against such desecration.

When I was finished, Fröhler made his appearance: he confirmed publicly the things I had said at the university, and proceeded to describe in detail how the events I had referred to had all come to happen. He told us how he had met Erwin Janik at the end of the war—where he had been sitting, and exactly what he had been doing when the Americans had marched into the city. Fröhler spoke at length about Erwin's brother Emil, who, even back then had a very controversial reputation. Then Fröhler said that it would take a bigger "freedom fighter" than Janik to get him to believe the "tale of resistance" Janik himself had told. The audience burst into laughter and applause—and the camera captured everything.

The *Heimatabend* ended late that night. I had enjoyed the performances; they had been astute and entertaining. The *Kabarettisten* had stuck it to those who had been anything but members of the resistance, and the effects of their satire reached far beyond Passau without passing it over. I liked this style.

My husband felt less comfortable than I did; he had sat facing the exit the entire time, fully prepared for any potential unpleasantness to erupt— especially when right-wing youths could be heard outside yelling Nazi slogans. He had more or less expected them to crash the place. Liegl had tried to reassure him, telling him that they had locked and secured the door just in case. He found this anything but comforting: my husband turned white as a sheet and admitted that, had he known there was no way out he certainly wouldn't have come. I wasn't sure whether he was joking or not. Neither was he.

The next day my life continued as normal, yet something was different: in a few weeks I would have to appear in court. Now I had to start collecting incriminating information to justify statements that had been, in the end, a defense of that person's character. The situation was absurd! Now Fröhler, too, was being sued. I visited Dr. Gantenberg and showed him the court order. "But he *was* 'brown!'" he said, and told me again about how much he had feared him back then, and about the discussions they'd had about the path Emil Janik had chosen with regard to the Nazis. He spoke about the difficulties he had had to face afterwards and about the conditions under which he had continued to lead his youth group—he always made sure that word reached Janik too late for him to impose any countermeasures. Dr. Gantenberg told me that he knew of yet another surviving witness to the activities of those days. His name was Nikolaus Fessler, and he could give me detailed information about his experiences with Dr. Emil Janik. If I could get this man to testify it would be the end of any debate about Janik and his relationship to the Nazis. If I wanted to make this happen, though, I could not go on defending Janik's character, since Fessler's statement—in combination with his, Gantenberg's, own— would be diametrically opposed. "All in all," Dr. Gantenberg finally remarked, "if Emil Janik took part in any kind of resistance, then it was against those of us who were in the *real* resistance." I had visited Dr. Gantenberg a few times in the past and heard all kinds of breathtaking things from him. But never had I heard him judge someone with such severity. His voice was full of contempt and bitterness.

The next morning I began my search for Nikolaus Fessler. In Niedernburg I'd had a teacher once, for biology and art, named Pia Fessler. She was a nun with the Maria-Ward Sisters. She must have been close to retirement even back then; she and another nun were the only ones in the convent who had ever dared to wear a short skirt and only "half" a veil (*einen "halben" Schleier*). Could there be a connection there? I had called her up once two years before when I had come across the name Fessler in some old documents given to me by Dr. Gantenberg. The documents had to do with a Passau attorney, Josef Fessler, who had been the only one to continue defending Jews into the 1930s—mostly against dispossession of their property and actual physical attacks—even though the laws no longer protected Jews against such things. Dr. Gantenberg said that Josef Fessler had been a shyster (*Winkeladvokat*) who took on "unimportant" cases, someone who defended "unimportant" people for small sums of money, and who had also "refused to refuse" providing services to Jews, with the explanation that "Jews were people, too," and it was only right to help them when they needed help. Josef Fessler was under observation by the Gestapo and the SD (*Sicherheitsdienst*). He was known as an opponent of the Nazi regime.

When I went through the registry in the city archives of Passau I found that an official file existed on one Josef Fessler. I immediately requested access to it. Unfortunately I was unable to see it, since it had reportedly gone missing. Only the empty folder was still there, I was told. I quickly became suspicious; too many times had I received answers like these. Whenever a file seemed particularly interesting it was "unfortunately" missing. Now I was fed up. I knew I was being lied to, but I didn't know what to do about it. And I needed this information for the chapter of my book titled "Resistance and Persecution among the Bourgeoisie." As if the possibilities for researching this subject weren't limited enough as it was—I couldn't simply switch my focus and talk about some other subject instead. At the same time I didn't want to give the impression that everyone in the bourgeoisie, of which my family and I were members, had been "yes-men" (*Jasager*). I believed that Dr. Gantenberg knew more than he was letting on. And I had always wanted to get the scoop on Josef Fessler. His name was not in the phone book and it seemed that nobody remembered anything about him.

At this point I remembered my former teacher. I called her, as I mentioned earlier, and asked her point-blank if she were by any chance related to the attorney of the same name. She reacted passionately; she told me about the various types of harassment her father had been subjected to. Yes, she said, he had defended Jews, and he had also done many other unconventional things. She herself, however, had been abroad during those days, and therefore, unfortunately, couldn't provide me with any details. I should call her sister, she said; she lived over in Hals and she'd know more.

Now I recalled Sister Pia: I wondered if she might be related to Nikolaus? It turned out that Nikolaus was her brother; he still lived in Passau. I called him as well. I briefly told him about the lawsuit and about Dr. Gantenberg. Nikolaus Fessler came to visit us at our home. His demeanor was very serious as he told us about the unbearable harassment he and other young people had suffered.

Chapter 6

THE FIRST BOOK

IN JUNE OF 1983 my first book, *Resistance and Persecution in Passau from 1933 to 1939*, was published. Everything happened as planned—almost.

Martin Hirsch made the trip to Passau to introduce the book at the *Scharfrichterhaus*. It was the first time that my father, who had been the president of the Diocesan Council for many years, had ever entered this building. My uncle, who was director of the Institute for Continuing Education for priests in Freising, just outside Munich, was also there for the first time. Sigi Zimmerschied, Passau's *enfant terrible*, who was also sitting at our table, asked the two of them playfully: "So, I hope you have noticed that I do not, contrary to what you may have heard, have horns growing out of my head." My mother, in the meantime, was "keeping guard" over my two children, just as she had done so many times before.

The *Scharfrichterhaus* was overflowing with people, and not even the *Passauer Neue Presse* was observing the internal ban on media coverage. Martin Hirsch was the evening's celebrity guest. He talked about how we had met and how impressed he had been with my manuscript. He made it very clear that he didn't have the slightest patience with anyone who wanted to take me to task for what I had written. He also announced that he was aware of the blackmail attempts and the legal threats I had received, and that he personally would defend me if necessary. Smugly yet with full confidence in his position, he added that he was now officially an attorney and that he was used to dealing with these kinds of procedures from his long years of experience as a constitutional court judge. "I've fried much bigger fish than some of the lawyers here," he concluded.

Then it was my turn: I started to read a few passages from my manuscript and noticed that the publisher had altered my words. Entire passages were missing, and others had been rearranged to become almost unrecognizable. I was almost frozen with horror. The audience didn't seem to have noticed, however; they applauded loudly when I finished and then began asking their questions. After I had answered some of the questions, I started to leaf through my own book, overcome with a feeling of uneasiness: could it be possible that I had given answers different from what had ultimately been printed in "my" book? I noticed, among other things, that the photographs were missing.

Martin Hirsch came back with me to the house and we stayed up late into the night. He reassured me that nobody would sue me, of that he was certain. For a few nights I didn't sleep very well, but it turned out that he was right: for six full weeks nothing happened at all. There were no more anonymous death threats, no lawsuits, no complaints.

Just a few things worth mentioning: there was a photograph featured in my book, taken in 1923, that showed the faces and names of the Passau members of Hitler's National Socialist Worker's Party, the NSDAP. My publisher suggested we have it enlarged to poster-size, fold it up, and add it to each book as an insert. Impishly he said, "That way people can hang it up above their beds either because they are proud of it or because they recognize a 'nice' enemy. And those who it makes feel awkward can just throw it away." I thought it was a great idea, and agreed to it right away. A small, local opposition paper to the *PNP* printed the poster on a two-page spread, and discussed my book at length. Almost immediately thereafter people began showing up at my doorstep, complaining about the "incredibly stupid" advertisement: well, yes, *of course* they had bought the book—they wanted to see if I had said anything about them or their relatives—and that's when they had found the poster! And *of course* they had taken the opportunity to remove the poster then, without another word, because it was possible, indeed *probable*, that one of their innocent children might some day discover the book on the shelf, and, out of idle curiosity, begin reading it unsuspectingly. But now that these innocent children had seen the advertisement and recognized the names of their grandfathers, or even in some cases their fathers, they had gone straight back to the book, taken it down from the shelf, opened it, and found no poster. And then they had become suspicious and started asking questions about their hometown's "brown" past. . . . And now! Well, now all these questions were "out in the open." Hadn't I considered that something like this might happen?

I wouldn't describe myself as gloating (*schadenfroh*)—at least not in the strict sense of the word—but I was very glad to have provoked such questions. I was also glad that I was apparently not the only one interested in our local history. And I was surprised how many people—even here in Passau—had bought and read my book.

It was reviewed in the magazines *Der Spiegel* and *Stern*, and even the ZDF (Zweites Deutsches Fernsehen, one of the main German television stations) did a report about it. The first printing of two thousand copies sold out within just a few months, this even though only one bookstore in Passau had agreed to carry it. All others had boycotted it. It was extremely amusing to watch and see who the first people to buy the book were: as soon as the first copies had become available a well-known editor in chief sent one of his employees, Peter Hutsch—ironically the very same Peter Hutsch who had earlier called to apologize to me for signing the complaint brought against me by his employer, the *PNP*—to this particular bookstore. He was instructed to buy two copies as soon as possible, but not to tell anyone who he was actually buying them for. Hutsch was similarly amused: he went straight to the manager and told him exactly why he had come and for whom he was buying the two copies. And to top it off, perhaps as an apology to me for his earlier behavior, he requested that the bill be made out directly to the editor in chief.

In the end, more than a few of those first people to buy the book would, just as they had feared, find their names printed inside. For I had written about the Gestapo and named quite a few of Passau's "brown sheep" in the process.

Chapter 7

THE COUNTER-REFORMATION AT
KOLPING HALL

NOT TO BE OUTDONE, the Catholic Church in Passau very quickly
arranged for its own event on the topic of *Resistance in Passau*. Prelate
Georg Teichtweier, who had been an acquaintance of my family for a long
time, was asked to speak. As soon as I saw the posters I knew that I had to
go: the whole thing reeked of "getting even" with me and the facts I had
publicly stated. I had learned from my experience at the university that
this time I would need to have reliable and competent witnesses there to
protect me against the things that would almost certainly be said about
me; I asked both my parents to go with me. They were prepared to shield
me against what might be said, as well as potential physical violence.
When the three of us entered Kolping Hall together, my parents were
flooded with greetings; old acquaintances from conventional social circles
filled the aisles. Many of the older ladies—my mother included—remembered
Georg Teichtweier from their youth. There were many of my parents'
colleagues in attendance, as well as several priests, among them Bishop
Franz Xaver Eder. My father ostentatiously introduced me as his daughter.

I sat down—a parent on each side—and prepared to take notes. Teichtweier was greeted with tremendous applause. He spoke about the heroic
actions of the Passau clergy during the Third Reich. There had been
nothing—he claimed—to tarnish this image. In vain I waited for him to
mention just one of the many, many disgraceful and grave transgressions,
for which mountains of proof existed.

Not one word was mentioned about the years of craven fawning before
the brownshirts. And there was not a word about the treacherous activists
and deceitful Gestapo informants who existed among Passau's Catholics.

I could hardly bear to listen.

Suddenly Georg Teichtweier abruptly changed the subject, launching
into an aggressive defense of the upstanding character of the long-serving

editor in chief of the *Passauer Bistumsblatt*, Dr. Emil Janik, deriding any claims to the contrary as "mean-spirited slander" and "foundationless character assassination." It wasn't difficult to guess whose claims he was referring to. My parents sat next to me, spellbound. A resounding applause arose all around us. Many people jumped to their feet out of enthusiasm. The bishop was the only person who didn't comment one way or the other. He sat very quietly, hanging his head—in the midst of the applauding priests.

I had my one and only chance to speak when Dr. Teichtweier invited questions from the audience. I politely asked if he perhaps knew what had happened to the two Jews who had been denounced by two priests in 1936 and subsequently imprisoned in the Passau county jail, after which they disappeared without a trace. The comment unleashed a storm of outrage. Not against the denouncers, mind you—but against me, who had dared to mention such a thing. Everybody was shouting. A CSU Municipal Councilman got up and demanded that I identify myself. His request was ludicrous: everyone there knew exactly who I was. I had been notorious for a while now. But I stood up anyway and told them my name. My mother was appalled to see the hatred and to witness the attacks being directed against me, simply because I was thinking against the stream and had dared to pose such a delicate question—a question that, in such polite society as this, was, quite obviously, unwelcome.

I received no answer. Dr. Teichtweier refused to accept what I had said. "No comment" was his only response. The CSU Councilman accused me of slander and character assassination; what I was suggesting could not possibly be true! He challenged me to name names. I informed him that I was bound by law not to do so. He immediately accused me of lying, of simply having invented the whole thing. Otherwise, he appealed, I would surely be able to provide such details. Several flustered people were yelling "Liar!" I told them that the documents proving what I had said could be found in the State Archives and that the *Passauer Zeitung* also had reported on them, in 1936. The mood in the hall was getting more and more hostile, the shouters increasingly malicious. Finally, I blurted out the two names. The hall grew silent. The dismay was palpable. I named Max Tremmel, who had been organist at the cathedral and was *Ehrenbürger* of the city of Passau, and Dr. Josef Enthofer, who had been director of a seminary and was still active in the Marist Cloister in Altötting, a place of pilgrimage. Both were highly respected citizens of Passau.

Dr. Teichtweier maintained he knew nothing about what had happened to the two Jews. After the event a few dozen people stayed to talk to Dr. Teichtweier. My parents and I also went up to him. My mother introduced him to me and showed him some of the newspaper articles Emil Janik had written. Although reluctant at first, he began to read them. My mother told him what really had happened that night at the university. Dr. Teichtweier listened to her—and finally formally apologized, right there in front of everyone. He said that Erwin Janik must have given him false information. Erwin Janik had telephoned him, asking him to defend his dead brother, Emil. I had badmouthed him at the *Scharfrichterhaus*, Janik had said; he had not mentioned anything about the university. Teichtweier also didn't know that I had only used the expression "brown Emil" while quoting someone else, and only while I was defending Emil Janik. Teichtweier also had no knowledge of the articles Emil Janik had written. Once more he apologized to me and to everyone present; he had done me an injustice. Of course I was not to blame for anything.

Franz Mader, who used to supplement his income and bolster his image by contributing occasional pieces about local life to the *Passauer Neue Presse* and the *Passauer Bistumsblatt*, overheard what had just been said. To make sure of this, my father pointed it out directly to him again. Despite everything, Mader ended up writing an outrageous article in which he accurately quoted all of the accusations that had been made, but failed to mention both the context in which they had been spoken and Dr. Teichtweier's apology. In his article Mader also made it known that the bishop was considering legal action. Nothing, no retraction, nor any number of letters to the editor, could undo what had been done. And certainly nothing of the kind was ever published.

My father later spoke both to the vicar general and to the bishop. The bishop made it abundantly clear that Franz Mader had acted entirely on his own accord—without his prior knowledge or consent. The entire affair was embarrassing enough as it was, he said, and he did not want to stir things up any further.

In the meantime, Professor Dr. Peter Steinbach, the Chair of the department of political science at the University of Passau, had sent me a written invitation asking me to visit. He had been so outraged by Janik's lawsuit that he had sent not one but two letters to Dr. Teichtweier. I quote:

Dear Mr. Prelate—

I deeply regret having missed your lecture on Church resistance to the Nazi regime in Passau. I would have been very interested in the subject, . . . not in small part based on information I have that it is connected with a less-than-justified and, to me, very regrettable legal battle between a Passau student and the editor in chief of the *PNP*, Dr. Erwin Janik. At my request, the student, Ms. Rosmus, came to see me during my office hours; I had attended a lecture by her here at the university, which had impressed me with its circumspection. The person with whom I spoke was not a member of the "younger generation" who felt exempt from all the dangers of German history, rather this was a young student who spoke with a great distinction about the resistance movement as it relates to various groups, from the SPD to the churches. She painted an impressively balanced and unbiased picture of the many outstanding examples of clerical resistance in Passau. Never before have I heard a twenty-year-old speak with such understanding and consideration on the topic of resistance. To my horror, I became aware of the fact that one of Ms. Rosmus's passages concerning Emil Janik, a passage which was in my estimation informed and fair and which, in its essence, had been exculpatory, had become the basis for a lawsuit. I subsequently asked Ms. Rosmus for permission to read her essay. I found it to be accurate and equally well informed, neither calculating nor a diatribe, i.e. conscientious and extraordinarily instructive, and therefore very fruitful. And then I was shocked to read in the press that the legal battle, instead of dying down, would seem to be escalating. Ms. Rosmus did nothing to deserve such treatment and I am very disappointed to see that a spirited young person must go through this kind of experience. I must confess that the series of events has challenged the limits of my credibility. It would now seem that, considering the rapid escalation of the case, an agreement is out of the question; in the meantime, however, another question has surfaced: it is the more general question of the limits on what researchers may freely claim in their work. And so I predict that a very fundamental legal debate has been opened up here, the effects of which may ultimately involve even the *Bundespräsident*, who served as the organizer of the contest in which Ms. Rosmus made such an impressive showing.

As a professor, however, I am also concerned about the person targeted in this way, in this case my student, Ms. Rosmus. How can we complain about the disillusionment of young people with everything from the government to political parties and churches if we continue "breaking butterflies on a wheel" (*dass mit Kanonen auf Spatzen geschossen wird*), or if a leading newspaper editor uses his position to manipulate facts to the detriment of others. I am therefore following this development with great concern, all the more so because Ms. Rosmus comes from a sheltered life and a respected family and has been greatly distressed and harassed. In all seriousness, could she have intentionally wished this upon herself? Especially considering the given topic and the character of Ms. Rosmus? After all, when we are dealing with the general subject of resistance, we are not talking about the justifications or the incrimination of single individuals—nobody is looking to institute public denunciation or de-Nazification, least of all Ms. Rosmus. Instead, the attempt is an analysis of the conditions for capitulation or resistance, of clearly grasping the costs of not having the courage of one's convictions. But then again, who among us can claim to never have faltered during this long, lonely time, which began in 1933? This is Ms. Rosmus's concern, and for this very reason it cannot be said that she ever "accused" anyone of anything, rather she simply described, reported, explained. I ask you to do your part in seeing to it that this matter is resolved amicably, for the sake of a young person, her family, and her future, but also for the sake of her credibility and ours.

Very sincerely, Yours, Peter Steinbach

As a result, Professor Teichtweier was no longer a witness in the suit, but Erwin Janik had not changed his position in the slightest. And the problems soon began for Professor Steinbach. A lawyer's son threw stones at his son on his way to school, and his wife received anonymous threatening calls. Finally the professor asked me to please understand if he decided to "keep out of it" in the future. Thinking against the stream is sometimes hard, but swimming against the stream is that much harder. In terms of its more far-reaching effects, not much came of the trial, but in Passau it was sufficient, yet again, to cause a scandal.

Chapter 8

THE COMPLAINT BEFORE THE
ADMINISTRATIVE COURT IN REGENSBURG

BACK IN KARLSRUHE, Martin Hirsch had asked me whether I had finally been given access to the documents I had been requesting for so long. I had to tell him no, neither the Episcopal nor the municipal archives had budged an inch. The City of Passau had been simply ignoring me and my requests for months. Hirsch looked at me with astonishment and asked why I didn't just sue the City of Passau. I had no idea such a thing was even possible. I didn't even know I was allowed to sue the city, much less what would be officially required to do so. Martin Hirsch must have noticed my confusion. "Just go to the administrative court," he said. "Whenever the authorities do not respond within a reasonable time period you simply request a court order compelling them to do so on the grounds of administrative inaction. All authorities have to respond to such an order, one way or the other. If they don't, you can sue them."

He gave me a long, questioning look. I was being confronted with a decision I had not realized I would have to make. "You can earn a lot of respect that way, and most likely you will win," he continued. "There's almost no doubt about that. But you certainly won't make any new friends that way. You will be hated in Passau—and feared. But it's up to you to decide what you want. Because once you've made that first step, your future in Passau will have been decided."

It was much clearer to him what would happen than it was to me. But one thing was clear to me: I wanted the truth. I wanted to know what really had happened under the Nazis. I wanted to get access to the files that, first for absurd reasons and then for no reason at all, had been kept from me. Martin Hirsch had a big smile on his face when I asked him, "And how do I go about filing a complaint?" He nodded triumphantly, as if he had just won a major victory, and told me I only needed to make a copy of my correspondence with the City and to mail it to him. He would also need to get his hands on the statutes and regulations, and the charter (*Satzung*) of the municipal archives. He and Diemut Majer would draft the petition for me. All I needed to do was send it. The term *Satzung* was foreign to me; I didn't know what that was. Nor did I know where I was supposed to send the official file of complaint.

Martin Hirsch was truly amused about this and said, "Only in Bavaria! If I didn't know where you were from before, I'd sure know it now!" Then he asked, rhetorically more than anything else, "So, I guess they don't teach you these kinds of things in Bavaria, do they? I suppose they don't give lessons in school on how to fight transgressions by the State and the authorities, right?" He was still laughing and shaking his head when he took me to Diemut Majer, who finally drafted the petition for me and told me that all I had to do now was to send it to the administrative court in Regensburg. I thanked them both profusely and was already looking forward to the day I would see the files. That was on January 13th, 1983. I had been waiting in vain for three years by that time. But yet another year would pass before anything happened: the City received my complaint, but the cultural committee (*Kulturausschuss*) would have to be the ones to make the decision.

The *Kulturausschuss* decided, almost unanimously, to deny me access to the files.

Only Friedl Volkholz, an SPD woman, and one other member voted in favor of my request. The CSU and the remainder of the SPD were united against it. The City argued its case based in part on information provided to them by Franz Mader, although he never appeared before the court to verify the information. The City also claimed that the documents in question were "personal" records, and thus confidential. Yet I could prove that the files I had requested were merely papers *relevant to* Max Moosbauer, papers that, according to the city's own charter, I was entitled to see thirty years after his death. The city promptly responded by increasing the statute of limitations to fifty years—this despite the fact that his relatives had already given their consent to my publishing the documents, and despite the fact that I was assured I would be given access to the same files in the Federal Archives in Koblenz, provided they were on record there, and despite the fact that the BDC, the famous Berlin Document Center, had also granted me unimpeded access to similar files.

The official hearing in my case took place on February 1st, 1984. My uncle, Dr. Walter Friedberger, had come all the way from Munich in case

I needed a witness. The regional paper *Mittelbayerische Zeitung* and the national *Süddeutsche Zeitung* sent reporters: this was the first time in the history of the Federal Republic that a "girl" had sued a City in order to gain access to Nazi files. The reporters watched the proceedings, sitting on the edge of their seats in anticipation of seeing a legal precedent set. If I were to win it would open the floodgates for innumerable similar requests.

I arrived by myself. I knew my files, my requests, and my rights. I was able to follow the arguments; the right to freedom of research and freedom of teaching granted in the constitution applied to me as well. I had kept all the deadlines for submitting my requests; the City had not. I had fulfilled all the requirements; the City had provided false information, and I could prove it. I had learned my lesson when it came to following the courage of my convictions. The City's official legal advisor and lawyer, Joseph Gevatter, claimed to know nothing of the consent of the Moosbauers, the policy of the Federal Archives, the BDC, or much of anything else for that matter.

The three judges finally declared that they were unable, even after extensive review of the files, to find anything that warranted confidentiality. And since the National Archives, the higher authority on the matter, had granted me access to even more sensitive files, a mere municipality could not reasonably refuse. The fifty-year rule was struck down. And the City's claim that I could possibly use the information irresponsibly was deemed unsubstantiated.

Joseph Gevatter made a final appeal, citing the impact this would have on upcoming local elections. The presiding judge took this fact into consideration, and suggested a compromise settlement: the City would grant me the files for my research and, to help assuage their concerns, I would let the City review the product of my research, my manuscript, before publication. This would be a win-win situation, the judge said. The City would save face and I would get immediate access to the files, preempting any delay the City could cause by filing an appeal.

We were granted a short break to think it over. I was torn. The important thing here, I was warned, was to reach a ruling; after all, this was a precedent-setting case, and only a clear ruling could serve as a basis for other researchers like myself. I understood the seriousness of the matter. My actions could pave the way for all future research in such cases. That meant that Martin Hirsch wouldn't have just been helping me out of this mess, but countless others as well. He would certainly be happy about that. On the other hand, I had now been waiting over three years already and didn't feel like waiting even another few months, or even years. I wanted to read the files. I weighed the decision over and over in my mind, trying to take everything into consideration. The question hinged on whether the decision would be broad enough so that the consent given by Max Moosbauer's relatives would be irrelevant. I had been given it, but would others receive, or be required to receive, similar consent for their needs? Would the judgment not, to a great extent, be based on that very point? When the judges returned, Joseph Gevatter agreed to the compromise; I considered everything again—and gave my consent as well.

The national press gave this case extensive and detailed coverage; the local *Passauer Neue Presse*, however, pretty much ignored the whole thing.

Chapter 9

NEUENGAMME AND THE DEATH THREAT

AS A 1981 KÖRBER Foundation essay competition prizewinner, I was invited in the summer of 1984, together with a group of other young people from various European countries, to an event in Neuengamme, near Hamburg. On the grounds of the former concentration camp a memorial site with an archive and seminar rooms had been built. Each summer young people were invited there, where they worked as unpaid volunteers to help to restore the former concentration camp grounds. They lived in a communal setup directly on the site.

I was pregnant with my second child, and felt generally miserable, but I desperately wanted to take part. Shortly after I accepted the invitation, the newspaper *Hamburger Abendblatt* wrote a piece on the project and my participation in it, and shortly after that I received a death threat. "You may go there," it said, "but you will never get out alive." The letter also said that if I wasn't careful I would be dragged off to the gulag and never heard from again. This was by no means the first such threat I had gotten, but as a pregnant woman I knew I was now responsible for defending not only myself. I went anyway. My mother took care of my daughter and I informed the administration of the camp about the letters and the calls. They arranged for a night watch to be set up in the commune. Two or three of us were to stay up for a few hours at night, taking shifts, to alert others in case anything happened. Certain areas of the camp were floodlit, and every once in a while a squad car would patrol the area. But the place remained a wide-open target; there was no retaining fence, and the area was surrounded by trees and old brick structures where someone could easily hide.

During the day we learned how to reproduce old photographs of the infamous "mountain of shoes" (*Schuhberg*) from Auschwitz. Back then, part of the "mountain" had been transported to Neuengamme, where the prisoners had been forced to make new shoes from the leather. Many children's shoes were among them. Maybe it was because I was pregnant at the time that I found this so incredibly distressing: I will never forget the sight as long as I live. With the help of the enlarged photographic reproductions we tried to pinpoint the original location of the *Schuhberg* on the camp grounds. When we had located some possible areas, two groups of us set out to begin test excavations. It was strenuous work, digging around in the rain and the mud, but not long after we began we had found the first remains. They were very well preserved. It was cold and wet outside in the open. Twice we had to dig actual drainage ditches to prevent our own trenches (*Betten*) from flooding. In the evenings, before crawling into our sleeping bags, we talked about what we now knew had happened, in part at least, back then.

On the third night it happened: suddenly the spotlights went on; we heard shouts. I was immediately wide awake. Two people had been keeping watch outside. A young man who had been sneaking around our tent had run toward us holding a butcher knife. Our guards were able to restrain him just a few yards from our tent. The police were called in to take him away. I never found out what happened to him. I never found out who he was. All I was told was that when asked about his motive he had said, "curiosity." He never said why he had been carrying a butcher knife.

Thereafter our daily routine at the camp continued: we searched for the remains of the crematoria and every so often ran into inmates from the local jail. They were on work release, and at night they had to return to the adjacent penitentiary. They mowed and weeded the lawn. Once we went to visit them. We couldn't believe our eyes: the building had previously been part of the concentration camp, and the chores performed by the current prisoners were the same as those performed by the "prisoners" back then. One inmate who was incarcerated because of tax evasion told us that he understood fully why he had to be punished, but to be put in that place bordered on cruelty. Here one was reminded constantly of the fact that people had been tortured and most likely killed. Right here, under one's own feet! Right here, where his fellow inmates had recently been ordered to build a park, and where they were now cutting flowers and watering plants, and where once the Nazi concentration camp Neuengamme had stood. The inmate knew who we were and what we were doing there. He said that he wanted to read my first book, but told us that political books were not usually allowed in the prison; he would have to ask for special permission and then a decision would be made. I don't know whether he ever received permission or read the book.

Once, a group of us played a game of soccer against the inmates. The question of what may have happened right there only a few decades earlier, on the very lawn where we were now playing, weighed heavily on our minds. Later we found out that our food was being prepared in the former "prisoners' kitchen"of the concentration camp.

Toward the end of our stay we received visitors: a delegation came to gather ashes and soil from Neuengamme. We were to fill an urn, which was later to be buried, together with the ashes and soil from other camps, at Auschwitz. The event received television coverage, and for this reason some in our group decided to noisily boycott the ceremony. I, on the other hand, felt that the idea to gather ashes from the site was a very moving symbol and did not take part in the boycott. Instead I expressed my desire, which we had discussed among ourselves in the group many times, to see the old brick storage hall of the former camp, which was now falling into ruin, be restored, and I used the occasion to officially express our wish. I offered to help personally with this project. Whether the project was ever realized, I still do not know.

Chapter 10

DR. LAMM IN MUNICH AND THE SURVIVORS

I WAS TWENTY-FOUR years old and all set to continue work on my subject —and I still hadn't had the chance to meet a single Jew. From newspaper articles in the 1930s I knew that Passau's last synagogue had been destroyed over five hundred years ago—by order of "our" bishop back then. Nobody could or would tell me how I might manage to contact any Jews. I searched the Passau telephone directory but could not find any entries. Then I looked through the Munich telephone directory and found a listing for "Israelite Cultural Affairs Community." The address was given as well. Without knowing who exactly to turn to I wrote a letter addressed "To the Chairman." I briefly explained that I was trying to find Holocaust survivors from my hometown and was having problems. Nobody there knew anything about it, or so I was told. I also told him in my letter that I was searching for files, but the municipal archives had claimed that they were "missing"; I was at a loss, and I asked him to help me.

A short time later I received a letter from Hans Lamm, the president of the Munich Jewish Community. He invited me with my husband to visit him in Munich. We should come to see him at the Jewish Cultural Community Center, and he invited us to have a kosher meal with him. I couldn't believe my good fortune: for the first time in my life I would meet a Jew.

I didn't know how I would have to behave around him, how to act, what set of manners or customs to observe. I didn't understand the concept of "a Jew." I was excited but, as a German, a non-Jew, I was nervous. I didn't want to make any mistakes. All I really wanted to know was what had happened to our Jews in Passau, and I thought maybe Dr. Lamm could help me with that.

My husband was anxious: he had never met a Jew either. He also had no idea about what it meant to be Jewish. He was from Munich and recognized the address, but he had never been to the Jewish Community Center. He was terrified about the encounter, but he refused to let me go by there myself, and so he came along.

At the entrance we saw a police unit; there was a video camera mounted above. The door was quite narrow; we were searched and then our arrival was announced by telephone. My heart was beating wildly in my chest. A secretary led us into the waiting room. There were photographs on the wall showing Hans Lamm with former Chancellor Willy Brandt and other prominent people. They were taken at various awards ceremonies, some of which were honoring Lamm himself. After a few nerve-wracking seconds we met Dr. Lamm in person: he was a small, delicate man of about seventy. He was sitting at his desk, writing checks. When he became aware of us he quickly stood, apologized, and took us out to the restaurant.

He asked all kinds of questions about me and my husband and about Passau, about our families and my work. He took an especially close look at my husband. He then said that he was not at all surprised I was having problems. Unfortunately he couldn't necessarily be of much help; the Community didn't have any files on Passau. And there were no survivors from Passau among the community. He recommended that I should contact instead an old friend of his, Henry Marx, the editor of *Aufbau* in New York. He would certainly print an advertisement in that magazine, and I was welcome to tell him that Hans Lamm had suggested I call. He then gave me the address and promised to drop Marx a line himself, just to be sure.

Then he asked me, very abruptly, why I was doing this, anyway. Nobody was interested in such things any more. I was stunned. I tried my best to explain why people my age needed to know what had happened back then. I told him I also wanted to get to know the people who had to leave Germany back then—the ones who were still alive, that is. Lamm looked at me skeptically, almost sullenly. He told us that he himself had survived in exile, in New York. But he had returned immediately after the war. A lot had changed, he admitted. Since a recent terrorist attack on the Jewish Community there was constant police surveillance, day and night. Video cameras were running around the clock, recording people's movements or anything suspicious. Visitors were searched and admitted only after the visit was approved and they were signed in. A certain amount of fear had returned. But these were only casual remarks; he quickly turned his attention to the menu and began to explain to us the foods that we would be eating that evening. When we parted company later he invited me to call him again, in case I didn't get anywhere with the help of the *Aufbau*. But, he added, he was certain I wouldn't be needing him any more.

Right after my return to Passau I drafted my advertisement for the magazine. It read something like this: Wherever you may be living today, I'm asking for your help. I am looking for information about Jews in Passau, but have been refused access to official documents. I included this ad in a letter addressed to Henry Marx and asked him to print it. I never saw the announcement when it ran, but within a few weeks I had received several letters: one from Robert Klein in San Francisco, another from Ilse Greenbaum in New York, yet another from Paula Pick in Haifa . . . all of these people were from Passau and all of them were available to give me information immediately. With no strings attached. They all gladly offered to answer any questions I might have.

I began very carefully: I didn't want to bring up painful memories, nor was I sure about what would be considered appropriate to ask. Letters were sent back and forth, sometimes several per day. The more answers I received the more curious I became. I asked some very personal questions: I wanted to know about their feelings, their hopes and dreams and their fears; I wanted to know what pained them and why.

After a few months I felt I knew them as well as possible without ever having met in person. We had never exchanged a single spoken word; I couldn't afford overseas telephone calls at the time. But I knew what made them tick. We had become confidants, although we were living thousands of miles apart, even though they belonged to a different generation and practiced a different religion than me. They now spoke a different language from mine and had a different passport. Yet I felt so close to them. I felt a part of them when they told me about their childhood, when they described their emigration and the difficulties that came with beginning a completely new life. I cheered when they told me about how they had succeeded and cried when they told me about the countless humiliations they had suffered. I grew furious when I thought about how nobody back home in Passau cared about them. I could not believe that no one had ever suggested they return. Still, I didn't understand when some of them openly admitted that they missed Passau!

Paula Pick had to break off correspondence after just one letter. When she had read my questions it became immediately clear to her that she had overestimated her capacity to deal with these issues. She told me that to have to give an honest answer would have killed her; she barely managed to survive then, and ultimately had to repress all her memories in order to simply survive. My questions would bring back everything and she didn't have the strength to relive everything again in her thoughts. She gave me her full permission to read her files, if I ever found them, but implored me not to ask any more questions of her.

I wrestled with myself on this: of course I didn't want to cause her any pain, but who else could tell me what had happened, who else could tell me about her family? I decided not to ask her any more questions. Years later I read her files. I researched them and sent her a copy of my book *Exodus*, in case she wanted to see what I had done with the material. When I was in Haifa and decided to visit her, she had already died.

Paula Pick was the only one who wasn't able to answer my questions. All the others did, some of them over the course of several years. I'm sure that I must have asked many naive or even absurd questions during that time. Since I didn't have a clue about Judaism, I wanted to get to know these people well enough to be in a position to tell their stories to others, so that I could take a stand for them. I'm sure that my questions got on the nerves of more than a few of them, and I'm certain that a few of them more than once shook their heads at my ignorance. But they all were incredibly patient with me; some even became good friends.

Hans Lamm, too, became a friend of mine. He offered to coauthor the book about the Passau Jews with me. He invited me to the celebration at the Saur publishing house in Munich, when they introduced a volume with a selection of his collected essays on the occasion of his seventieth birthday. I was "very pregnant" at the time, and he asked me to name my child after him, if it were a boy. He himself had no children. He said, half jokingly, that I already had one and I should give this one to him. It was his honest desire to help with the education of this child as long as he lived, to care for it as if it were his own. He was the first one to congratulate me on the birth of my daughter, Salome. She would have learned to love him but only a few months later he was dead.

I was in Passau cleaning the sink when my mother-in-law from Munich called and happened to mention in passing that he had died. My husband had answered the telephone and when he heard the news, called out to me: "Lamm has died! They announced it on the radio." I was paralyzed, speechless. I sat down on the edge of the bathtub and began sobbing uncontrollably. My daughter Nadine had just turned three. She came up to me and tried to console me. A short time later I received official notification. I had learned in the meantime that Jews didn't place flowers on a grave; but when I visited Dr. Lamm in the hospital a few days earlier he had been very happy about the birds-of-paradise I had brought him. I didn't want to say good-bye to him without a symbol of the deep connection between us. I went to Munich with a bouquet of birds-of-paradise in my hand.

At the cemetery there were dozens of police with their squad cars, transmitters, and weapons forming a barricade. I was allowed to pass unchecked and made my way down to the memorial service and the grave. There were politicians, reporters, and cameramen in the midst of masses of people. I couldn't hold back my tears. Again and again strangers offered me their condolences; apparently some of them thought I was a relative. Ernest Landau approached me and introduced me to Max Mannheimer. The latter immediately offered to help me in any way he could, should I ever need it. He had wanted to "jump into the breach" for Hans Lamm. But there was nothing anyone could have done at that point to help me. For weeks after the funeral I was in pretty bad shape. Never before had a death affected me nearly as much as the death of Hans Lamm. And never before had I felt the loss of another human being so deeply. I put away all his letters and postcards so I wouldn't constantly be reminded of him.

One year after the funeral Jews erected the gravestone. One of Lamm's former colleagues called and asked me if I would give the memorial speech. I was desperate: I couldn't even think of him without crying, much less imagine having to write or speak about him. I asked that she please understand, but I didn't have the strength at present. His colleague was indeed understanding, but she also managed to set me straight: Hans Lamm had wanted *me* to speak. If I didn't speak, someone he was never really fond of while he was alive would speak instead. I should at least spare him that, she said; after all, he could no longer fight his own battles. I knew she was right, but I had no idea where I was going to find the strength. I gathered myself and told her that I would do it.

For the first—and so far last—time I went to see my doctor to ask him for a tranquilizer. A strong one. He did not understand my reasons, it seemed, but I received the pills anyway. I was to take one in the morning and a second one right before leaving the house. I did just as I was told, but the pills had no effect. So I took another one, and yet another, and then a third one. When I arrived at the cemetery, my speech in one hand

and the few remaining pills in my pocket, Charlotte Knobloch approached me. She was Lamm's successor, the new, charming, and attractive president of the Munich Jewish Community. Her mother had not been born Jewish, therefore she was considered non-Jewish by the orthodox Jews. But so far she had been accepted as a Jew by the majority of the Munich community; after all, they weren't orthodox, they were merely conservative. Charlotte Knobloch took me aside and informed me that if I were to speak the orthodox part of the congregation would make a point of leaving the cemetery. She assured me that it had nothing to do with me as a person, but that it was because of the fact that I was a woman, and because I was not Jewish. She was obviously embarrassed by the situation and immediately proposed a compromise. In order to observe proper form, one of the official representatives of the Cultural Community would speak at the grave, and my memorial speech would be printed in the community publication, in accordance with Lamm's wishes. Back then I didn't understand the motivation of the orthodox Jews; after all, everybody knew that Lamm and I had been good friends. But, to be honest, at that moment they would be lifting a great weight from my shoulders by relieving me of the duty to speak. I immediately agreed to the compromise. I was saved by the bell. Charlotte Knobloch seemed equally relieved. I really had no idea how I could have held back the tears.

Max Mannheimer, however, was offended. He felt that this was a major affront against me and threatened to step down from the board of the Community if the orthodox members didn't formally apologize. He asked them pointedly how some of the Jews could complain about a lack of interest amongst the non-Jews if they simply pushed aside people like me. No apology came, and Max Mannheimer made good on his threat.

Of course, had I been in his shoes I would have done exactly the same thing. I, too, would have been extremely ashamed for my community. I too would have distanced myself from such an embarrassing situation. But my relationship with him and other Munich Jews was already sufficiently close as not to be burdened by it.

The Munich Jewish Community Paper didn't mention anything about the incident. It simply printed my (undelivered) speech:

For Hans Lamm.

We are gathered together here, once again, at the grave of Hans Lamm, to dedicate a memorial for a friend. Until about a year ago Hans Lamm spoke for me. Today I speak for him:

Hans Lamm did for me *everything* one friend could ask of another, right up to the very end. He helped me to think in political terms, to work historically and to feel as a human. Hans Lamm was a fellow traveler (*Wegbegleiter*) and mentor. He taught me to show understanding and tolerance while still standing up for what I believe in—in short, to go my own way.

In my attempts to shed light onto the past of my hometown of Passau during the Third Reich, and in this way to contribute to the reconciliation and the peacemaking process with the Jews, I have become the target of incredible hatred and had to face almost insurmountable difficulties. Hans Lamm not only strengthened my resolve, he also helped me directly: he vouched for the validity of my research and helped me to find material. He made it possible for me to get to know Jews and to understand Jewish thought, and in doing so helped to create an understanding and a trust that serves as the foundation for our continuing cooperation.

Hans Lamm was one of the few people who supported me and my work from the very beginning. I could always rely on him, in spite of all the difficulties, and I could count on his help in any situation.

I will never forget when I visited him in the hospital for the last time—he was already close to death—and he asked me once again how *I* was. Then he got up, took up a pen, and wrote one final letter to one of my most vociferous enemies in defense of my work.

And just as he shared the pain with me he also shared the joy: it was perfectly natural for him to send me a telegram at five A.M. in order to be the first one to congratulate me for winning the Geschwister-Scholl Award.

He took care of me like a father. And this dear friendship is a major reason why my daughter bears the Jewish name Salome. Many people could not understand how I, a young German woman, could do this to her, and my doing so resulted in much hostility against me. For me, the act is a symbol of German-Jewish communication and reconciliation, something Hans Lamm has advocated all his life.

Today, as his friends are dedicating his gravestone, I see in this stone a reminder: Hans Lamm taught me to stand up for truth and justice, whether it's convenient or not. This principle didn't win him many friends; nevertheless, when I find myself facing difficult situations, I still ask myself what *he* would have said, how *he* would have reacted. For me personally, Hans Lamm's heritage also means this: that my book about the Jews of Passau—which we had planned together—was completed in his spirit and as a memorial to him.

Chapter 11

ON TOUR WITH HANNE HIOB

I HAD BEEN BACK from Neuengamme for a while when Hanne Hiob called. She is the daughter of Bertolt Brecht. She was a ballerina as a child, before becoming an actress, and had for many years been notorious for her skillful productions of so called "political spectacles." Her name, however, didn't ring a bell with me in those days. She said she had read about me in the newspaper and wanted to use me in one of her productions. I had to admit to her that I wasn't familiar with her productions. It's quite simple, she explained: now, forty years after the end of the war, it is time to remember all the groups that had been wronged. Because to this day most people had not received any restitution.

She said that she foremost prized diversity: homosexual children's book authors, a lesbian couple who were pastors, a communist and former concentration camp prisoner who had shared the stage with Brecht, Sinti and Roma singing "modern" gypsy songs—and me. She wanted me to talk about the problems I had run into during my research. A completely new world was opening up before my eyes. In the conventional Passau I had grown up in, I barely knew that people like these even existed.

Regarding Sinti and Roma, I remembered that in the late 1950s my mother had taught gypsy children. A few of her colleagues had refused to teach these DP classes. My mother didn't know that DP stood for "displaced persons" and that the term referred to all the people who earlier had been abducted by Hitler's henchmen and were still being treated like garbage. But she had felt sorry for the little children who could barely speak German. They were frequently unwashed, and sometimes they stole an apple from a tree on their way to school and offered it to my mother: my mother would remind them about God's commandment, "Thou shalt not steal." But she could not stay angry at them. She went to these classes voluntarily and the children showed their thanks through their attachment to her.

They lived on Danziger Strasse, the street that ran parallel to ours, where the homeless shelters were. Everybody avoided them. I had been there only once, as a child, with my mother. It was the day of my First Communion at church. I had received all kinds of presents and my mother asked me which one was my favorite. I pointed to an amber pendant that had a small snail fossilized in its center. My mother asked me if I thought that Gaby would like it as well. Gaby was one of my classmates. She lived on Danziger Strasse. Of course she would like it, I said. My mother suggested that I put the pendant back into its package, wrap it back up in pretty paper, and take it to her. I was confused, but I didn't dare argue.

Looking back I realize how much this experience meant to me: before then I hadn't understood that there were houses in my hometown where the windows were broken out and there was no heating, no carpets, no real furniture. Holding my mother's hand I walked up the dark, cold staircase to where Gaby lived. The door was open. My mother was greeted with some embarrassment, but with friendliness. Gaby joined us. I gave her the present and she was very happy. I have thought about the look on her face many times since: the expression of amazement, of not understanding *why* I was doing this, *why* this gift was now hers, just like that. Her dark eyes were open and trusting. Gaby and I had been going to school together for three years at that point and I had never been paid much attention to her. She was a skinny girl, inconspicuous. Neither smart nor stupid, neither ugly nor pretty. I didn't know anything about her. Back then I had no idea why my mother would choose her, of all people, to give a gift to. My mother and I left a little while later. What remained was the memory of the cold, somewhat "creepy" building—and Gaby's soft, distantly happy eyes. Homeless shelter . . . Danziger Strasse . . . gypsy children, the words rang strange in my young ears back then.

And then, just as Hanne Hiob was telling me about her tour, I remembered a potential obstacle: I was pregnant. Still, I definitely wanted to be part of it. My husband was fuming; why was I even having anything to do with people like that? But I was curious . . . very curious, in fact. I wanted to know about these gypsies. I wanted to hear what their music was like. I wanted to know about Esther Bejanaro and the songs she and the concentration camp prisoners sang back then during the days of the NS resistance; I was curious about the homosexuals who would appear on stage and talk about their love, about the discrimination they faced, about the life choices they had made. I wanted to meet a real friend and colleague of Bert Brecht. I had first read Brecht in high school when I was about fif-teen or sixteen years old. I had read his *Stories of Mr. Keuner.* I was fasci-nated by his plays; I remembered how there had been a bound edition of his collected works in my father's library. The thought of seeing some of his works performed on stage, directed by his daughter and another friend from East Germany (the German Democratic Republic, or GDR), was immensely appealing to me. I was eager to meet Peggy Panass, who had observed and reported on NS trials for many years and who was nearly destroyed by the work. I was curious to meet Erwin Geschonnek, the old communist who, at the end of the war, had been crammed into the ship *Kap Arkona* with thousands of others and sent out to sea. He was one of the very few survivors (and a recipient of the State Medal of the GDR); later, while working as a journalist, he had described his experiences in the book, *Sinking of the Kap Arkona.* He would be speaking in the production about this tragedy and his research.

The dress rehearsal took place in Munich; I was blown up like a bal-loon and could barely sit, but I watched, transfixed, until the very end. I loved the way Hanne Hiob read, played, and sang Brecht. With a combi-nation of tact and harshness she criticized the way minorities are still—or better said, once again—being dealt with in Germany. Carefully and systematically she chose places that deserved perhaps more attention than others: there was the notorious city of Nuremberg, where Josef Mengele had repeatedly holed up after the war without being touched by the authorities; there was Hamburg, where Günther Schwarberg, the well-known and popular journalist, wrote about children used by the Nazis in medical experiments, in the *Children of Bullenhuser Damm.*

The long performances on stage were followed by lengthy conversa-tions backstage. There I had a chance to observe these "others," to ask them questions, to get to know them and to learn to respect them. There was one characteristic they all had in common: they knew exactly where they stood, they knew precisely what they wanted, and they stood up for it in public. They were all able to make it clear to perfect strangers what it was that made them "different" from others and why they planned to stay that way. I learned a lot during those evenings and I took part in the tour as long as my ever-expanding belly would let me. I only cancelled once, shortly before my due date, so as not to put my child at risk.

Chapter 12

THE GESCHWISTER-SCHOLL AWARD

AFTER MY BOOK HAD been out for a few months my publisher called: somebody from Munich had asked to receive a couple of review copies. He had read the article in *Der Spiegel* about the book and was a member of the jury for the Geschwister-Scholl Award. He was very excited and asked me if I knew about the award. I told him I knew nothing, either about the award or about the person who had called. My publisher told me that the prize was awarded once a year, for moral courage in literature (*Zivilcourage*). It was awarded by the Bavarian Publishers Association and the City of Munich; the jury consisted of a group of independent and highly qualified people who also nominated the candidates. Up to then only very famous literary figures had received the award—and they had all been men.

Rolf Hochhuth received the first award for his book *The Deputy;* he was followed by Rolf Fühmann, Walter Dirks, and Reiner Kunze from the GDR. And now, perhaps, me. He asked me not to mention it to anyone, so as not to jeopardize the whole thing. I couldn't believe what was happening and told only my parents about it. Weeks went by. Then, out of the blue, I received a phone call: Armin Eichholz wanted to meet me and see what I was like in person. By then I had gotten used to all sorts of unsolicited calls and requests. Sure, I said, come on by. He arrived in the company of Ute Fischbach, an editor for the *Münchner Merkur*. As I always did for such guests, I baked a dessert, made coffee, and then sat down to answer all kinds of questions about the book. Questions such as: "When I was reading your book I noticed that it was written in two different styles using different idioms; why is that?" They were pointed questions, but the man asking them seemed pleasant enough. I answered them as best I could, politely, perhaps even patiently. My "patience" may have had something to do with the fact that I was pregnant and my usually quick reactions had been slowed a bit as a result. "Journalists!" I thought to myself.

A few weeks later the phone rang. It was not yet six o'clock in the morning and I was still half-asleep: it was Father Michael from the Capuchin monastery, *Mariahilf*. He had often preached at the cathedral. I had frequently gone to *Mariahilf* because I had particularly enjoyed his sermons; they were different than all of the others in town. But why in the world was he calling me at six in the morning?

"Congratulations!" I heard him say and then, again: "Congratulations to you!" I had no idea what he was talking about, I thought he must have dialed the wrong number or something. He had never called me before. Perhaps he wanted to speak to my father? Before I could reply he continued: "I just opened up the paper and saw the news." He wanted to be the first in Passau to officially congratulate me. He told me I had won the Geschwister-Scholl Award, to be presented in November in Munich. My head was spinning. I hadn't heard anything about this. Then I remembered my publisher; he had mentioned some award; but that was months ago.

As always in situations like these I went to see my mother. I told her about the call and then looked through her paper. And there it was: the news about me winning the award—for my book *Resistance and Persecution*. I didn't understand why I hadn't yet heard about it myself. More calls came pouring in—more congratulations. As well as more attacks. I was both the first woman to receive this prize and the first person the same age as the Scholl siblings had been when they were executed by the Nazis—all previous, and subsequent, recipients were rather "more mature in years." All were writers and had received the prize for their prose or their poetry. And me? I had just turned twenty-four and was by no means a poet.

Only once had I made an attempt to write poetry and then only under duress: I was eighteen years old and it was the end of November. My German instructor came up with the crazy idea to have us write a poem about Saint Nicolas. I couldn't stand Saint Nicolas stories in the first place, much less the cheap morality kids were forced to swallow about being "naughty or nice." Plus, I had not the slightest talent when it came to poetry. I was not a very imaginative person. And as if that wasn't bad enough, the teacher also demanded that we write our poems about the person sitting next to us! The whole thing amounted to us "informing" on our classmates. I hardly knew the girl who sat next to me at the time, at least not personally. There was absolutely no way in the world I was going to be forced to write something so judgmental about her, and then perhaps even present it in front of the entire class. I felt like I was going to explode. Did the teacher really believe that seventeen- and eighteen-year-old students would start ratting on each other, and in front of their teacher of all things? Or did he think that we would simply flatter each other so that nobody would end up looking bad? And the thing had to rhyme too! Well, he could count me out, that was for sure.

The others found the idea absolutely hilarious, at least those who expressed an opinion on it. Most of them immediately began writing, like good little students. Not me. I was still trying to find a way out of this mess when the teacher leisurely reclined in his armchair and began to read the paper. Apparently the lesson was over as far as he was concerned. That's when I had my "imaginative" idea, one he would only grow to appreciate years later: I'd participate. I decided to behave myself and rhyme as reasonably as I could. I'd show him what it really meant to "inform on" someone—in a pleasant, rhyming, literary form. I would be sure to include both positive *and* negative traits. I pushed myself in my chair out into the aisle slightly, to where I had a clear view of the teacher, and then proceeded to write my "poem." But it wasn't going to be about the person sitting next to me.

I tried to make it as personal as possible without stepping on anyone's toes. (That type of thing is not difficult in a small town where everybody knows everything about everyone else. My teacher's wife, for instance, had been in a group class my mother had taught; his mother had a greengrocer's where my grandmother used to shop.) I described him sympathetically, because I liked him and respected him, but I let a certain criticism shine through, in gentle and rhyming language. Just as he had asked. It turned out to be a relatively long poem. I wasn't surprised when, at the end of the hour, he asked for a few contributions to be read aloud. I wasn't even surprised that he expected me to read mine. He was very surprised, however, when he found out I had written about him. He became embarrassed and his face turned bright red. He seemed to tense up; he took his glasses off and started blinking nervously. But he did allow me to finish reading. At the end of the class, as he was collecting our poems, he asked, smiling, why I had done that. Not long ago he told me that he still had my poem. So much for my career as a poet.

And now, exactly six years later, I was to receive the Geschwister-Scholl Award. My name was to be placed next to names such as Reiner Kunze. I was delighted, honored, but something didn't feel quite right when I thought about it. I could see being placed in the same company as Rolf Hochhuth, maybe, but he was a troublemaker, he wanted to "get even" with society publicly (though in a highly refined way, of course). That was not what I wanted, nor was I even capable of doing so, in my opinion. My name next to the names of the Scholl siblings? My experiences comparable to theirs? Mine had been bitter enough, but there was no comparison with what they had suffered. I had only risked ruining my reputation as an upright, respectable member of the bourgeoisie—they had risked their lives. I had lost an image—they had lost their lives. They had attempted to mobilize the masses in order to put an end to Hitler's regime of terror— I just wanted to know what had happened in my hometown. They had stood trial at Germany's infamous *Volksgerichtshof* because they had wanted to build a more human society, a society in which Jews, Russians, and many others could live as respectable and respected citizens. I had been in court because a local editor in chief felt like he had been insulted and had decided to sue. I wasn't convinced that I necessarily deserved to receive this award.

But then I heard the news that this had been the first time in the history of the award that the jury had agreed unanimously on the winner. I heard that even the members of the CSU faction in the Munich cultural committee had voted for me—credit my father's reputation for that. When I heard that Inge Aicher-Scholl, the sister of the two Scholls who had been executed, had endorsed the choice, as had the other family members and the survivors of the legendary White Rose (*Weiße Rose*), all my doubts evaporated. These people were sure to know what they were doing. Now I was simply curious about what it would all be like. I wanted to meet the relatives and learn more about Hans and Sophie Scholl. I was eager to understand the criteria for the award and to meet the members of the jury. My body, on the other hand, was not cooperating—I kept getting bigger and heavier. My official delivery date was only a few days away and I began to doubt whether I would be able to accept the award in person. Armin Eichholz reserved a seat in the first row for my gynecologist, just in case. Dietrich Strothmann from *Die Zeit* dropped by during that time for an interview. When he saw me he joked, "My how you've *grown!*" Annette Ramelsberger, who had been a classmate of mine and since become a journalist, asked to interview me as well.

Finally the big day arrived. I drove to Munich. I had been invited to the Publishers' Round Table and was seated next to Klaus Piper, who told me I needed to get set up with the German Author's Union (*VG Wort*), who would help collect the full royalties on my books. Klaus Saur, who was president of the Bavarian Publishers Association at the time, gave me one copy of each book in his current catalog as a present. I met Mr. Beckurts, one of the directors of the Siemens Corporation. He warned me about possible criminal and terrorist attacks that might threaten me in the future, and gave me advice about how to protect myself, such as taking a different route each day and to leave the house at varying times. All the precautions he gave me didn't end up helping *him* too much, unfortunately. Not long after our meeting I would find myself standing at his grave: he and his driver had been killed in a terrorist attack.

The award ceremony proper took place the next day in the Old City Hall. Martin Hirsch had made a special trip from Karlsruhe, accompanied by Diemut Majer. Hans Lamm had to cancel at the last minute. But my uncle was there, and so were my parents and my older daughter Nadine. Even the deputy mayor (*dritter Bürgermeister*) of Passau, Koniszewski, was in attendance. He was a butcher by profession and we had already been at loggerheads (*lagen im Clinch miteinander*) for a while by then. He had argued on television that if a Holocaust memorial were, in fact, necessary, surely it should be placed in the cemetery and not in such a conspicuous place, a public space where people tended to gather. I had argued for the latter.

The hall was filled to capacity, mostly with invited guests and journalists. Some of them started bawling loudly when I thanked them for their reporting and their support. I kept talking, though. Afterwards Armin Eichholz spoke. I was deeply moved by his speech. He said:

Laudatio for Anna Rosmus —

You may be able to tell from the baroque music playing that this is intended as a calming event. If this was a broadcast of the television news-magazine *Aspekte* you might have expected the musical background to be something like a contest between the "Horst-Wessel-Lied" and the "Internationale," broken up by a church choir, with Siegfried Zimmerschied providing the guitar accompaniment.

Something has become very clear to me for the first time in the short history of the Munich Geschwister-Scholl Award: we are not here to reward escapes into belletristics. To live up to its name, the award demands greater passion, something that reaches beyond the traditional boundaries of belle-lettres. It demands a degree of risk-taking. And so, ladies and gentlemen, you now find yourselves members of a jury that asks itself each year: what is it that defines an attitude of risk-taking in our day and age?

Does it mean sneaking into a company under a false name as Günther Wallraff has done? Or does it mean standing up on the downtown Munich central square, the *Marienplatz*, impersonating Christ and screaming "Shit!" at the top of one's lungs like the performance artist Achternbusch? After all, all of these people in this fully democratized land of ours are fully insured against libel. Or is it necessary for our prizewinner to come here from the GDR, so that finally we might have a real victim of persecution in our midst—even if only on loan?

And sometimes we have the sneaking suspicion, do we not, that we are stuck in the subconscious of our contemporaries, forced to deal with the old duty to feel smitten with remorse? Consider this, ladies and gentlemen: for those Germans under the age of fifty, the feeling is that the Federal Republic is overflowing with moral commemorations (*Gedenk-Anlässen*) they have inherited from their fathers. Most of them have been born into a system of negative battlefield celebrations (*Sedan-Feiern*), so to speak. And whoever among them is not ready—from a very early young age and while still an untrained worker in the field of mourning, to adopt as their own the conventional sense of dismay at Germany's past—of them it is freely said: they have understood nothing about history, they are in fact incorrigible, reactionary, and, in general, immature. But I digress before I've even begun. I simply want you to consider this: the Scholl siblings would be of retirement age today. But their prize is not reserved "honoris causa" for seniors who happened to survive some minor criticism. In a country with cultural sovereignty comprised of eleven autonomous states and thousands of awards, perhaps the only way to sound a call for the future that may actually be heard and taken seriously, is if the call echoes the collision of aesthetic and political fields of vision. Let me here recall the Frankfurt *Goethe Award* given to Ernst Jünger—which for some represented a politicizing of the "Olympian" Goethe by a poetaster from the far right. And I remind you of the Darmstadt *Büchner Award* given to Ernst Jandl—which for some meant the privatization of the revolutionary Büchner by a rhymester from the left center.

Dear Ms. Anna Rosmus, what does all this have to do with you, you may ask. Here we are, pulling you out of Passau and into the public eye, and mentioning your name in the same breath with those such as Hochhuth, Reiner Kunze, Franz Fühmann, Walter Dirks—each of whom could be your father or even grandfather.

And if you should ask: "What do I have to do with literature?" I would in all honesty have to answer: nothing—yet. But you shouldn't be intimidated by the term "literature." After all, we're dealing with the kind of a book award here where the purely aesthetic qualities do not take center stage.

As for the other challenge: there you have set your own terms. You were motivated to participate in a student essay contest on the subject of "German History" sponsored by the *Bundespräsident*. You then continued your search for the truth about Passau's history in the 1930s with a dedication that was preceded by the horror of disbelief. And there was the further horror upon discovering the fact that the existing literature on this period of history did not correspond with what people were telling you. And there was your conviction that what they were telling you was not sufficient. And finally, confronted with the doors of various archives anxiously closed in your face and with even more closed-minded people who had also closed themselves off out of fear, a final question occurred to you, a question you ended up having to answer for yourself: Why was everyone reacting so defensively? It was this persistent curiosity alone, originating as it did from a state of proven innocence, that has transformed a "good girl" from Passau into a political creature and now the creature is maturing and blossoming despite the resistance of conventional society.

In this way your book *Resistance and Persecution in Passau from 1933 to 1939* is also a book about aversion and denial. It is a book about memory. It reads like the exposé of a murder mystery. And it is different from anything thusfar written by those in the field—for various reasons:

1. It provides a well-researched and comprehensive account of the seemingly private yet already prepolitical behaviors exhibited during the era of National Socialism—an attitude represented by a typical comment quoted from a female sales clerk who said: "Well, we were just living our lives, we weren't much concerned with politics."
2. The book is not based on simple preconceived notions. Instead the author gives the impression of having stepped back in time and actually observed what was going on around her; as if she were learning an extinct language.
3. The people and lives she has reconstructed based on information from archival materials, splinters of conversations, questionnaires, etc., retain their fragmentary character in her writing; they retain a sense of incongruity, and reflect the cleft, the dichotomy in their

natures. In this way she stays within the immediate scope of an attainable truth.

In Passau more is now known about the workings of a predominantly apolitical community during the time of National Socialism. I am impressed by the way in which Anna Rosmus has sought out and analyzed long-forgotten facts—and without buying into the leftist doctrine of denouncing out of necessity all that is of the past.

It is not as the daughter of a chairman of a diocese council, but based on her research, that she recognizes the decisive role of the Catholic Church in the matter. In her work she observes that "farmers and the majority of citizens were traditionally 'black'; they remained faithful to the Church and were not much inclined toward National Socialism."

I would like to use this opportunity to ask a modest favor of the ladies and gentlemen who find themselves in disagreement with the unanimous vote of the jury. Please do not let yourself be distracted by the publicity surrounding this book, which was delivered into our hands by a courageous and bright-eyed young woman. Anyone who sees history anew through her eyes will better understand the younger generation.

One will also come to understand why Ms. Rosmus has become somewhat of an anathema to many Passau families. The archival materials, of course, lack some of the context. And there is some truth, after all, in the famous speech given by the 86-year-old Cato, who said: one cannot defend oneself before anyone except one's contemporaries. . . .

Ladies and gentlemen, were I to argue that Anna Rosmus has made history speak from within itself it would be almost equivalent to placing her, like a mascot, onto the lectern of this year's meeting of the German Historical Association (*Historikertag*) in Berlin. Because it is there that the professors, after an era of a purely sociological approach to their field—an approach which proved to be disastrous—finally rediscovered the human being as the creator as well as the victim of history. The old "micro-historical broom closet" was mentioned, which once again might offer a path toward knowledge. This theory, which ultimately has contributed to our new and intriguing sense of homeland, was confirmed by Anna Rosmus and her applied research. She is, scientifically speaking, the first woman to emerge from the historical broom closet, if you follow my line of thinking.

Dear Ms. Rosmus, I hope we did not tax your patience too much. Let me congratulate you as the recipient of the fifth Geschwister-Scholl Award.

You are now of the exact age as Hans Scholl when he was executed on February 23rd, 1943. And perhaps his name represents a burden to you. But there is so much that lies ahead of you. And I hope that you and your family will be able to truly live and work in accordance with the quote by Claudel, which Hans Scholl recited in his final letter to his parents before his execution. It reads: "Life is a grand adventure toward the light."

And should you find this statement too grand, I ask you to continue reading the letter to where it states, matter-of-factly: "It would be a good idea, if, in the future, we could learn how to tell each other less about what is going on in our hearts and more about what is going on in our minds." It seems to me that this has been your conviction all along. Thank you for your attention.

Armin Eichholz was right: a statement describing life as "a grand adventure toward the light" was too grand for me—back then. I was already living with threats upon my life, with hatred and envy, jealousy, and all kinds of curses directed against me. My life had little to do with "light." I was still very pregnant. I was taxed to the extent that I simply wanted to crawl into a hole just to have a few hours of rest. I wanted peace and quiet for the delivery, for the convalescence, and, eventually, for the continuation of my work. But there was not going to be much peace and quiet: instead dozens of cameras and spotlights were focused on me; I was expected to respond to Armin Eichholz's eulogy. I was expected to give my view of things: what I had done, and how, and why. . . . I approached the podium. Luckily there was enough room behind it for me and my belly. I stood there in front of hundreds of invited guests and I looked into their expecting eyes. It was my turn to speak.

I admitted to them how honored I felt, but also how humbled: my name next to those of the Scholl siblings—it seemed out of all proportion. My problems were ludicrous compared to theirs. They had paid with their lives for the risk they had taken. All I had done was to sacrifice my respectable image, my friends, my social status, and my previous way of life. They had the state against them, the law, the ruling majority; my enemies were just a few bitter old men, diehards, and cowards. The state and its laws had granted me the right and the opportunity to do what I was doing. Where I had needed help I had often received it—in spite of all the difficulties. All this had been impossible for the Scholl siblings. I admitted my unease at receiving the award, and thanked the many people who had contributed to my success. My words were met with applause, compliments, and flowers—again, quite different from what had awaited the Scholl siblings.

The reception was kept reasonably modest. I was escorted to the *Ratskeller* restaurant located in the basement of Munich City Hall. During dinner I had the chance to meet the jury and was told that Professor Broszat, director of the Institute for Contemporary History in Munich, had been especially supportive of me. I was seated next to Klaus Bismarck; one of the most charming dinner partners in all of Munich, Armin Eichholz assured me. He was right. I got to know Klara Huber and Inge Aicher-Scholl. My parents were very impressed by Dr. Schmorell, the son of the executed Alexander Schmorell. "He looks exactly like his father," I thought to myself. I immediately took a great liking to these people, even though I didn't know very much about them. The feeling turned out to be mutual. I came back every year to attend the Geschwister-Scholl Award ceremony. I also returned every year to commemorate with them the anniversary of the murder of their relatives. Only after some time did I notice that there really were two "wings" of the group. One was progressive, as Franz Müller had been; its aim was to help to make certain that what had happened back then would have measurable consequences and that the public would learn from it. The other was the more conservative one, centered on the figure of Alexander Schmorell; its aim was to honor the dead by holding an annual commemoration. Back in 1984 I was not aware of the fact that the two groups generally did not agree on the award recipients. I suppose that, at the time, I represented a compromise of sorts.

Chapter 13

THE ASSAULT IN MUNICH

MY SECOND DAUGHTER was born a short time later. I again received anonymous death threats. Somehow the news that I would be needing another C-section had leaked out. The caller promised me that I would receive enough anesthetic so that neither I nor my child would survive. At this point I was used to this kind of thing and reacted fairly calmly. I did, however, mention it to my doctor. He made sure that certain security measures were taken in preparation for my delivery. The other rooms all displayed the name of the patient in it outside the door; my tag was left empty. The nurses were advised not to let anybody come in and had to announce everyone who asked for me. While I was still on the IV drip and unable to move, somebody had to occupy the bed in my room, while I was hidden behind the curtain.

Nothing happened. But immediately after I delivered my daughter and it was reported in the *Münchner Abendzeitung* that I had named her Beatrice Salome Kassandra, fresh calls came in: how could *I*, as a *German*, do such a thing? What was I trying to do, increase her chances for deportation to the concentration camp?

A few weeks later I was scheduled to appear in Munich to hold a reading from my first book. The event was well publicized. There were posters everywhere, and all the newspapers were writing about it. And not to be outdone, more threats accompanied the publicity. Threats against me if I dared to appear, threats against the organizer if he went ahead with the event, and threats against a journalist if she dared to report about me one more time—even the police received a call. When I arrived, two police vans were waiting outside and policemen were securing the area. Visitors were being patted down and forced to have their handbags checked.

I felt awful. Just like in a kitschy mystery novel, I thought. Then somebody pointed out to me all the places where police were stationed, in case I needed help. How ironic, I thought, to be holding a reading about resistance and persecution in a situation like this. The audience seemed pet-rified, and I was honestly relieved when the event was over. Exhausted and tired I went home and straight to bed. A day or so later, I would learn, a troop of neo-Nazis demolished the theater in which I had spoken. The guests there were indiscriminately beaten up, furniture was smashed to pieces in a fury of blind rage. There was a reasonable explanation: the organizer told me that the poster advertising the event had listed the wrong date for my talk.

Chapter 14

THE CSU CITY COUNCIL AND THE HUNDRED PAIRS OF UNDERPANTS

HEINER LICHTENSTEIN WROTE IN the magazine *Tribüne:*

> Excitement has returned to Passau, once again thanks to Anna Ros-
> mus, whose book *Resistance and Persecution in Passau 1933–1939* sent
> shock waves through the pious cathedral town (*Domstadt*) three years
> ago. The young amateur historian and recipient of the Geschwister-
> Scholl Award . . . has recently written an essay entitled *Suffering of
> Passau*, which appeared in the anthology *Do You Love Germany* and
> resulted in a CSU city councilman suing her for slander.
>
> The CSU councilman's chances for success are not very promis-
> ing, however, as the defendant was able to prove the historical truth of
> her allegation with the help of documented evidence stating clearly
> that the Jewish clothes salesman was indeed denounced by the two
> priests.

Ulrich Chaussy commented on the events in the New York *Aufbau:*

> Passau 1936. Two gentlemen of the clergy turn to the Gestapo. . . .
> Through their denunciation the two priests avoid payment of a "trou-
> blesome" laundry bill for one hundred pairs of underpants. The horror
> story the Gestapo hears, from a dignified and trustworthy source, is a
> clear confirmation of what they already know from their (twisted) Nazi
> ideology. Passau 1986. Today, nothing would be known of this event,
> which happened fifty years ago, if it weren't for Anna Rosmus. . .
>
> Now Mader is suing Anna Rosmus to the tune of 500,000 Deutsche
> Marks (DM) or two years' imprisonment unless she removes every
> mention of him from her essay *Suffering of Passau*. He is not only
> attempting to rescue the honor of the clerical denouncers from 1936,
> at the expense of their Jewish victim; now this denouncer of the 1980s
> wants to be seen as a victim himself.

Dietrich Strothmann of *Die Zeit* called again during this time to ask how the trial was going. He summed up the situation with his usual precision of intellect. Åke Williams also called from Sweden. He had read the *Aufbau* article and couldn't believe what was happening. How was such a thing possible, he asked?

During the war Åke, a Swede, had worked as a reporter in Berlin, together with Lars Hjörne. Lars was now the owner of the *Göteborgs Posten*, the largest newspaper in the south of Sweden. Lars wanted a story about this curious case and Åke was ready and willing to make the trip to Passau to get it.

We met at the Hotel Zum König; Åke wanted to see how the local people would react to me. We spoke for a few hours, about Passau, my work, my family. He needed some names and facts about the Mader case. He also wanted some photographs of me, including one of me sitting at my writing desk. When we entered my house we ran into my husband. Åke's horrified comment upon seeing him was: "Looks like you married the wrong one there." It was not clear to me back then why he had said that. I had no idea that, sooner rather than later, he would become one of my best and closest friends.

Shortly after Åke's visit the *Göteborgs Posten* published a full-page article about Passau and my work. It was planned as the first article in a series. Åke had struck at the heart of the matter and had become active in my cause: he inquired at the Office of the *Bundespräsident* about the government's view of the case; he wrote to various authorities and asked for statements; he wrote in such great detail about my case that I received many invitations to Sweden. Swedish television came to Passau and produced an excellent report about the Mader case.

Various journalists had announced that they would be present in court on the day of the trial; Åke had even phoned ahead to ask that a seat be reserved for him. But it soon became clear that this trial was not going to take place: the court informed the press that the presiding judge had fallen off his ladder while picking apples and was not able to show up in court. And there was nobody else to preside in this case.

The conservative *Passauer Neue Presse*, as expected, mentioned nothing about this. Only a brief note appeared saying that the trial had been moved to January 22nd, 1987. At that point, the district court of Passau would move to prohibit me from talking about the case further, threatening me with a fine of 300,000 DM if I disobeyed their order. Naturally, it never came to that either. Ironically enough, that very same afternoon yet another journalist announced himself, saying that he wanted to discuss the case with me. He didn't sound very trustworthy to me, but he was extremely persistent, and so I finally agreed to his visit. This "journalist," however, acted so strangely when he arrived that my husband asked him to leave our house that very minute. The man finally apologized and made a confession that took me completely by surprise: he wasn't a journalist, he was actually Franz Mader's son-in-law! He had wanted to somehow get a look at my documents to assess how incriminating they were. And then he proceeded to ask me if I were willing to call off the press, as his father-in-law was perhaps prepared to retract his complaint. According to him, the court had suggested he do so.

He was most concerned, however, with the negative publicity. I told him straight out that, even if I wanted to, I could not help him. Several of the documents I had were already circulating among the press.

Swedish readers were informed that the trial never took place because Franz Mader had retracted his complaint. Readers in Passau did not hear anything about it: The *Passauer Aktuelle Zeitung* had been forced to close down and the leading *Passauer Neue Presse* did not report on it. The case was soon forgotten. It was only three years later, when Michael Verhoeven included a scene about this episode in his film *The Nasty Girl*, that hundreds of thousands of people would laugh out loud about the abrupt and bizarre conclusion to the trial. Again and again the question came from incredulous journalists and moviegoers whether this was not just a bit overdone for effect. No one could believe that things could have actually turned out the way we said they did. In Sweden it was rather a different story.

Chapter 15

THE NEW GUY

THERE WAS STILL VERY little known about the history of the Passau Jews. I still had not been allowed access to many of the files. All along, though, I had known that the entire research process would be a race against time. Therefore, on January 5th, 1987, I wrote another letter to the City:

> *Herr Oberbürgermeister* (Dear Mr. Mayor)—
>
> Not long ago it came to my attention that Mr. Arndt has been commissioned by the City of Passau to undertake a project entitled "Sudeten Germans in Passau," and is receiving the cooperation and financial support of the employment office in his efforts. I would like to pose the following question: Would the City of Passau be willing to take on a similar project with the theme "Jews in Passau"?
>
> The long history of the Passau Jews offers at least as much material; it can be stated with relative certainty that the Jews had at least as much influence on the city as did the Sudeten Germans. A larger number of people and personalities, people who distinguished themselves in public life, have come from within the ranks of the Passau Jews than from the latter group. In terms of its economic, cultural, and political significance, the "Jewish aspect" in the history of the city of Passau is of at least equivalent importance and certainly no less interesting than that of the latter group.
>
> I hope you will consider this proposal very seriously, and I request your response as soon as possible, in order to make it possible for the employment office to act on its behalf.

It took three years to hear back from them, in spite of my repeated inquiries. Only after the reunification of Germany in 1990 did something finally happen: The City had finally commissioned a temporary position for the project and had "hired" a chemist from the GDR for the job. The problem was, he had no idea about Passau or about our history. Dr. Brunner (the cultural councillor), however, was apparently quite pleased with his choice; this way, he claimed, one didn't run the risk of the person being negatively predisposed.

The *Passauer Neue Presse* reported in grand style about "the new guy." It listed the trips that had been planned to various archives and it said that the research would subsequently be published as a book. One year later the man had hardly come up with anything, and even the second year brought few results. Many years have now passed since my initial application—without any noteworthy developments having occurred at all. The book was never published.

Chapter 16

DR. WURSTER STRUGGLES IN VAIN

THE MADER CASE MAY have been closed for the courts, but the talk about it in Bavaria was far from over: Dr. Wurster, the archivist of the Episcopal Archives, finally saw his opportunity: The *Passauer Bistumsblatt* of February 15th, 1987, published his opinion piece with the following headline: "Not Responsible for Jewish Deaths: Public Accusations against Prelate Max Tremmel and Dr. Josef Enthofer Prove Unsubstantiated." And about Dr. Enthofer he wrote: "This deeply religious man and most benevolent priest must have experienced great pain from such accusations, particularly given his well known inability to deal with worldly matters. Dr. Enthofer had merely interpreted the behavior of Fabian Heitzner as a confirmation of the kinds of accusations made against the Jews by the propaganda of those days . . . Prelate Max Tremmel had had similar things to report in his initial statement."

When he had seen the comment, "Released," Dr. Wurster had concluded that both Jews had actually been set free! As if that made it alright.

My uncle, Dr. Walter Friedberger, had been a student at the seminary at the time that Dr. Enthofer was director there. My uncle was the kind of man who weighed his words very carefully, someone who was fully aware of the consequences of what one says. He generally preferred to remain silent than to incriminate somebody. But when my uncle read Dr. Wurster's article he became furious. He spoke about how even the youngest pupils at the school would do their best to avoid Dr. Enthofer— something that had been previously confirmed by another colleague, the priest, Dr. Hermann Gantenberg. They all had expected that he would "tell on them."

That's when I became enraged, and on February 11th, 1987, I wrote the following open letter to Dr. Wurster:

> Well, it's about time that you expressed yourself on the topic of the relationship between the Passau Catholics and the Jews during the

Third Reich, Dr. Wurster—even if it's only in the *Bistumsblatt*. In your article you spoke about the "scientific verification" of a file that you had in no way verified, but merely looked at. It is true and "scientifically verifiable" that I have read the archival file. Also true and scientifically undeniable is the fact that the priests actually *did* denounce the Jewish men. But it serves neither truth nor science if somebody like you comes along and starts to twist the facts as you once again have.

Why do you take such pains to deliberately conceal significant parts of the truth? You write that the priests had not been acting "out of their own free will," but had "been manipulated." But is the way in which they were "manipulated" supposed to remain a secret? Mr. Enthofer stated for the record: "While the salesman was showing me his samples and throughout our negotiations, I noticed that with his right hand he was stroking my left hand, up and down, in a constant rhythmic motion, so that I had the impression that, by doing this, the salesman aimed at gaining a certain hypnotic control over me. And while I do remember everything that was happening exactly, I believe that this manipulation on the part of the salesman was intended to influence my free will and decision-making power." And Tremmel said, "I cannot believe that I was making a decision based on my own free will when I was signing the agreement." Are you embarrassed by these details in any way? Or are they simply the honest truth? You hardly incriminate these Jews by describing just how harmless they actually were! Even you admit that "violations of the laws against treachery (*Vergehen gegen das Heimtückegesetz*) were usually punished with the utmost severity." Was Mr. Enthofer's "well known inability to deal with worldly matters" to blame for his inability to recognize this obvious danger? Are you trying to imply that their judgement was indeed impaired at the time of signing, or do their actions not show that the two priests reported "the Jew" in full awareness of the consequences? To be sure, why else would he have made it a point to say: "I had the impression that the salesman was a Jew." And why, if the priests' sole intention had only been to cancel the contracts, would they include in their complaint certain economic and political information? A simple charge, or even just the threat of such, would have been sufficient. What other choice could these Jewish men, as "racial outsiders" (*Rassenfremden*), have had than to simply cancel the contracts?

Instead the clergymen chose to lay it on. According to Enthofer, the Jew had "intentionally made false claims about the government during his various sales visits" and "pretended to know, for a fact, that another period of inflation in Germany was just around the corner, and that food ration coupons (*Fleisch- und Brotmarken*) were already being printed and would be introduced very soon." Tremmel gave a similar statement.

Aside from the fact that the Jewish salesmen had been telling the truth, the priests were supporting "brown" propaganda, had strengthened it by their actions, and even came up with their own version of racial vilification. The fact, that "the Jew" and his political statements were reported without any reason could also be called denunciation. Human lives had been put on the line, if not intentionally then through acts of gross negligence. The legal insignificance of the reports became evident immediately. Not even the Gestapo's nationwide dragnet operation had managed to turn up further incriminating evidence. And even if you, Dr. Wurster, claim to have found evidence of "a trail leading out of the Passau county jail," it hardly makes a difference to the fate of those victims. Do you really believe that incident mightn't have hastened their deportation to the concentration camp? Are you forgetting completely about the annexation (*Anschluss*) of Austria two years later, when the slightest excuse, such as the information included in the above reports, was sufficient to eliminate "unwanted elements" from society? Have you ever given a thought to their families, who were forced to live without an income thereafter? Have you ever considered what the two prisoners had to go through during those months? And even if it was nothing more than "simple" interrogations . . . would you consider this a welcome change for the persecuted? Is that the kind of treatment you consider to be appropriate for society's minorities (*Minderheiten*)? Have you, Dr. Wurster, ever thought for a minute about the meaning of human dignity?

I love these people, Dr. Wurster. It pains me when such minorities are made to suffer. When people are tortured without having committed any crime. When they have to suffer because no one will stand up for them.

I cannot change the fact that they were informed on and I cannot change their fate. But is it not time that the truth, the whole truth, be told, finally, in honor of their memory? Do we not owe them at least this?

I have done my best to find out what happened to them and met with great resistance in my attempts: the archives of the diocese remained closed to me for six years. I have publicly inquired after their fate during an event in the Kolping Hall—to no avail. I have asked hundreds of people to tell me what they know, in vain. I repeatedly asked Dr. Enthofer for an answer without ever getting one. I have repeatedly asked you if there were any mitigating circumstances but never heard anything more from you on the matter. Only one person told me he had witnessed the execution of his cellmates. I never quoted this person because I was looking for proof, more proof. Even the names of the priests, which you yourself have printed, I revealed only after I was repeatedly ordered to do so—because *I* respected the laws governing personal privacy.

Finally I would like to point out to you that I cannot be held responsible for what the national and international press choose to make from this incident.

Chapter 17

ROBERT KLEIN RETURNS

AMONG THE JEWISH EMIGRANTS who used to live in Passau, Robert Klein had been especially open toward me from the very beginning. His sensitivity and his vulnerability particularly endeared him to me. I asked him lots of questions and we corresponded frequently, sometimes with three letters going back and forth in one week between us—me in Passau and him in San Francisco. The more I found out about him the more curious I became. After some time he admitted to me in one of his letters how homesick he was. He also said that he was very apprehensive about returning to his former hometown of Passau: he had been back twice in the years shortly after the war in order to obtain some documents from the people who had "Aryanized" the shop that had belonged to his parents and who still owned it, but they had dismissed him. The Zacharias family wasn't going to hand over any documents to him, nor did his former classmates want to see him again. Robert Klein told me in detail how pathetic their excuses had been. It made me feel ashamed. I wanted to help him. I didn't know how, but I wanted to offer some emotional support. Carefully I pried further. I asked him about what had been especially meaningful and what especially damaging to him back then. "Back then," for him, was the year 1936, when he was forced to leave Passau and decided to emigrate to Palestine; "back then," however, also meant the time when he returned to Passau in the years directly after the war, as a visitor, and found himself facing closed doors. I wanted to be able to give him whatever it was he was missing back then—and was still missing now.

After a while it became clear to me that what he was most hoping for was some form of compassion, an interest in how his life had proceeded; a confirmation that it had only been the Nazis who had wanted to get him out of town, but that the people were on his side. That what counted for them was Robert Klein, the person, not the Jew. What hurt the most, I learned, was not the fact that in 1936 he was escorted to the train station by the *Oberbürgermeister* and told in no uncertain terms that his return would be unwelcome, but the fact that after the war nobody had asked about him, cared about what had happened to him, or asked him if he wanted to return.

Of course, how could anyone have known that he had emigrated, and since nobody had his address, how were they supposed to get in touch with him? No one knew whether he and his relatives had even survived the Shoah. Right after the war it was nearly impossible to simply track someone down.

True enough.

But what was their excuse in the 1950s, when he had returned and himself gotten in touch with his friends? All it would have taken then was an open mind—or an open door.

It was obvious that there was no interest or compassion for Robert Klein. I wasn't there myself and so I cannot speculate about the reasons why. All I knew was that he had been waiting for a sign. A sign that someone, anyone, was interested in him and in his life and cared about how he felt. He had waited in vain. Just as he had waited for some kind of financial reparation—as if it were possible to compensate with money what had been taken from him in terms of life, love, relationships. The more I got to know him the better I began to understand him: the money that he, as the heir of a successful clothing business, would unquestionably have been entitled to would have made so many things easier for him. For instance, he could have financed the numerous hospitalizations he repeatedly had to undergo due to his experiences during the Nazi persecution. Money also would have made it significantly easier for him to start his life anew, first in Palestine and then in San Francisco. But what he had been waiting for more than anything was some form of human response. It should have come from Passau, from the people he had known and loved. It should have come from Germans, in an attempt to help him get over what he had suffered at the hands of the Germans just a few years earlier and to give back to him part of what others had taken away in an act of brutality: a sense of home.

When I got to know Robert Klein he was seventy-eight years old and very ill. His first wife, Paula, who was not Jewish, had died. All his former ties to Passau had been severed—at least on the surface. He was nevertheless homesick. I didn't know what to do for him, how to try to make it up to him. I was twenty-six years old and non-Jewish, and I knew none of

86

his former friends or neighbors. I didn't know anything about his tastes or lifestyle. But I felt for him.

I decided to turn to the *Oberbürgermeister* and Dr. Brunner, the newly appointed head of the city cultural department (*Kulturamtsleiter*). I showed both of them his letters in which he spoke of his homesickness and asked both of them to invite him back to Passau as an honorary guest (*Ehrengast*). I thought it might be good for him to receive an official invitation. An official welcome by the new *Oberbürgermeister* might make up for some of the terrible damage done by his predecessor, the former *Oberbürgermeister*, when he had officially forced him out of his hometown during the Nazi era. I also thought it would be a gesture of goodwill if Robert Klein were not asked to pay for his own ticket and lodging. He had suffered greatly at the hands of those responsible without being guilty of anything. In addition, he and his parents had consistently been great benefactors of the City of Passau. They had donated clothes from their shop to needy Christian children for their First Communion ceremonies, food rations to soldiers: whatever the occasion, the citizens of Passau could always count on the generosity of the Klein Brothers—that is, until they were forced to leave.

I wanted him, at the very least, to be welcomed back into the city as a *guest*, even if Passau was no longer his *home*.

But my pleas fell on deaf ears. There was no money for that kind of thing, I was told. I thought back to the 1920s and '30s, when the Klein brothers would jump into the breach (*einspringen*) with their support and aid without being asked twice.

And now that Klein was an old man and in very ill health, and might have needed just such a gesture, no one was willing to jump into the breach for him. I thought about the millions of Deutsch Marks our city was spending on decorative lighting so that they could illuminate the Oberhaus Castle or the cathedral and supply tourists with promotional materials; I thought of the award given each year to a Sudeten German or Silesian who was a displaced person; I thought of the famous first-semester reception for thousands of students, financed each year by the *Oberbürgermeister*; I thought of the expensive trips our city councilmen took to France and Japan, which were all paid for from the City coffers. But apparently there was no money for Robert Klein.

You can imagine my annoyance when the *Oberbürgermeister* and the head of the cultural department informed me that all these funds had been budgeted—but that there were, quite simply, no funds for any Jewish "visitors." I was enraged when they tried to assure me that this had absolutely nothing to do with the Jews, that in no way did it reflect *any* resentment or *anything* of the sort—that there were simply no funds budgeted for such a thing. Never before had I been so fed up with German bureaucracy as I was then. For me it was not simply the usual tactlessness and insensitivity, it was an outrage! I thought about the death transports to Auschwitz, which were only possible because an entire chain of bureaucrats had worked hand in hand to make them possible. I thought of the excuses these people had later made in an attempt to prove their innocence in the murders: there were the so-called architects (*Schreibtischtäter*) who had simply organized everything from the comforts of their office desks, but who had never touched a single hair on a single Jew's head; there were the Party members who had taken the Jews from their houses, or guarded them after they had been collected, but they had never really killed anyone. There were the men who had driven the trains and were only doing their duty in doing so, but had otherwise had nothing against Jews. There were the Transport leaders (*Transportführer*) who were only keeping careful records and who had reported escapees, which had nothing to do with anti-Semitism, but simply with duty and scrupulousness. There were those who had decided, by simply pointing a finger, who would go to work in the concentration camps and who would go to the gas chambers; and even this decision was made according to strict, objective guidelines, based purely on who was deemed fit to work and who was not. There were those who had simply designed the concentration camps and the gas chambers, those who had simply built them as part of a more-or-less routine construction contract. There were those who had only managed the buildings and those who had simply been assigned to throw the Zyklon B canisters into them, yet never locked any people into the chambers. There were the ones who simply carried the bodies away, or simply incinerated them, just as undertakers did, in civilian life.

It was this attitude that drove me insane.

Because I didn't know how quickly or effectively I could have changed things to be of help to Robert Klein, I decided to look into one of the "budgeted" options to help get him back to Passau. And an option actually did exist, almost: Klein was a painter. Passau had its own city museum, which was financed by tax money. An idea was born in my mind! I tactfully asked Robert Klein if he would be interested in exhibiting his work in Passau. When he enthusiastically agreed I applied for an official grant for an art exhibit—to show his paintings. It was to take place in the Oberhaus, perched high above the roofs of Passau, and all the local dignitaries were to be invited to celebrate the opening. I wanted a reception with an official greeting and a clear and unmistakable welcome for the artist—and Jew—Robert Klein.

This concept was much more palatable to the *Kulturamtsleiter*. Of course, the current season was booked solid and the museum was closed in winter. It was impossible to simply cancel an exhibit and replace it with another. But I sensed another way. We soon agreed on the idea to, just this once, extend the season for about a month. The plan went over well with the City; after all, little extra money would be needed since the building belonged to the City and there would be sufficient personnel on staff. An additional reception, a few posters, a few invitations . . . it wouldn't cost the world. I immediately called Robert to ask him when he would be willing to come and whether he wanted to open the exhibit in person. He hung up on me without comment. I couldn't understand what had just happened: was he not happy? Or was he now regretting his decision? Did he not have the fortitude to come? And finally: how was I to explain to the *Oberbürgermeister* and the *Kulturamtsleiter* that now, after I had finally received their consent, the event really wasn't all that important anymore?

I was still rolling all this over in my mind when the phone rang: it was Klein, calling back. He told me that he had been so bewildered that he had needed a moment to sit down and consider things. Had he heard me correctly, was he really invited to come to Passau? With his paintings? He was overjoyed and so was I.

A few months later I was picking up Robert Klein at the train station in Passau. I asked the *Oberbürgermeister* to officially be there to receive him; and eventually he did so. There were others present to meet him at the station: there were many of Robert's former acquaintances; there were several classmates and neighbors, his father's chauffeur. They were all obviously very happy to see Robert again. For him all this was a great relief. He was delighted about the official welcome to his former hometown. Even years later he wrote in his letters that this had been the high point of his life.

I shared his joy. I never told him just how long and hard I had worked to put all this together; only years later did he find out that I had cheated just a little bit: it was in the year 1990, at the premiere of *The Nasty Girl*, the film about my early attempts to discover the truth about Passau during the Nazi era, in San Francisco. He was the guest of honor (*Ehrengast*) and was received ceremoniously. His eventual reaction to the film, however, was disturbing: when he saw the Passau cathedral and heard German he literally fainted. Throughout the entire night he needed oxygen. Memory had overwhelmed him.

For a few days I stayed in his guest room, listened to him getting up at night and falling out of his chair. It was awful to have to stand by helplessly, not knowing what to do. I listened to him and hoped that his physical and psychological condition would soon improve. But (again) my hopes were in vain.

Robert Klein died in 1993. We stayed in close touch up to his final days. The *Passauer Neue Presse* reported, briefly, on his death.

Chapter 18

JEWISH "EHRENGÄSTE"

AFTER THE SUCCESS OF Klein's visit I decided to invite other former Passau Jews back to Passau, and suggested to *Oberbürgermeister* Hans Hösl we invite Ilse Greenbaum from New York for the coming year. It was my hope that the *Oberbürgermeister* might now have a deeper understanding for such a gesture and that he would cooperate readily this time. . . . Far from it! We had to go through the whole rigamarole again! First the City refused to assume the costs for three nights in a hotel, not to mention the other travel expenses.

I had taken a liking to Ilse Greenbaum; her letters were very low-key and sensitive. I didn't want her to feel like a tourist when she returned to Passau. Finally the City "generously" offered free tickets for one organ concert and one visit to a museum; Rolf Henkel from the *Münchner Abendzeitung* sarcastically wrote: "Valuepackage: Three DM!" I thought the whole thing was simply outrageous and was determined not to stand for it.

An acquaintance from the Jewish Cultural Community in Frankfurt offered to wear his yarmulke and to come to Passau as a "journalist." As soon as Ilse stepped off the train he planned to make a point of asking me who was paying for the guest's hotel bill loud enough for the cultural deputy (*Kulturreferent*), Dr. Brunner, to hear, but not loud enough for Ilse. It was both of our hopes that the *Kulturreferent* would have a change of heart at the last minute, and what do you know! Dr. Brunner changed his mind at the last moment and offered to take over the bill in the presence of Ilse Greenbaum.

It was quite a different story with Ulrich Zimmermann and Michael Westerholz of the *PNP:* I had asked both of them to assist in the preparations for the visit and had supplied them with information about Ilse and her family. Both had immediately agreed to support the cause and reported on the event in great detail in the days leading up to it. They had also published my request for former neighbors and classmates to respond and submit their names so Ilse could see them again. Once she had arrived, two major reports followed: one of them was titled "Happy Reunion at the Cathedral" and carried the curious subtitle, "Former Bishop Antonius Hofmann and Ilse Greenbaum Were Former Schoolmates."

Michael Westerholz knew how to write a dramatic article. His began,

> Visitors of the cathedral were not the only ones in for a surprise yesterday: former Bishop Antonius Hofmann had just walked though the main entrance of the cathedral when he stopped and exclaimed: "Ilse?"; what followed was a moving scene: the two elderly people greeted each other with great agility, like two old friends who had a lot of catching up to do. . . . The bishop had recognized Ilse Greenbaum, a Jewish woman from New York who was born in Passau and his former schoolmate from high school in the Nikola Strasse, in recent reports and photographs. He had decided to send her a letter of invitation.
>
> In the cathedral they listened to an organ concert before the Bishop escorted her to his home as his guest for lunch.
>
> "He is completely unchanged; and his good mood is still as contagious as it always was," Ilse Greenbaum said joyfully.

Michael Westerholz also informed his readers that on the same day Ilse had paid a visit to her former neighbors, who back then had bought her parents' business and thereby actually made possible their departure from Passau. In fact *I* had taken Ilse to the location of the renovated store and introduced her to the new owner. Their meeting was slightly frosty, but Ilse felt it had been worth it. Michael Westerholz reported that "the Kreilingers showed her the business correspondence between their grandparents and the Greenbaums, and, in addition, numerous family photographs." I don't know for a fact if this is actually true.

I also accompanied Ilse to downtown Passau, where she met up with some former classmates of her deceased sister Margot. They sat in the garden together and leafed through old photo albums filled with childhood pictures. I took this rare opportunity to ask the ladies about all kinds of private memories: everyone had something to contribute. Never before had I witnessed such a reunion and never before had the difference between the New Yorker, Greenbaum, and the Passauers been so apparent, both visually and verbally. Never before had I realized the differences in their mentality as clearly as on that afternoon: Ilse was very delicate and glib, alert and full of energy. She looked just the way somebody might imagine a New Yorker should look: elegant, stylish and perfectly made up—beautiful and eloquent. The women from Passau, however, who had spent their entire lives in this town and who had never been forced to flee and had never wanted to live anywhere else than in this small town in Lower Bavaria, were quite different. They looked just like grandmothers straight out of fairy tales: old, round, wrinkled, and portly. But somehow still sympathetic, and even trustworthy.

Ilse was very impressive, and I was fascinated with her from the first moment I set eyes on her. She was a partner and an ally, at home at the Metropolitan Opera and at the New York designer shops, and her life had been full of excitement. She was constantly on the move, always in search of something new, always keen to fill her days with fresh experiences and not to miss anything. At the same time she was extremely pleasant and not the least bit arrogant. I liked Ilse a great deal. She reflected the type of life she had herself grown to love.

When we got back into the car in the evening she quickly said, "We are from different worlds, they and I, don't you think?" She was right, of course. After a short pause she added, "We are concerned about our appearances. That doesn't seem to be the case here. We spend a lot of money on the way we look, we take care of ourselves. When I imagine that I might have ended up like the others today, I must say that I'm glad that I left. I may not have had the more peaceful life. But I certainly had the more interesting one." A few days later Ilse Greenbaum left Passau, without a hint of sentimentality.

Westerholz wrote afterwards in the *PNP*:

> Just as she was preparing to leave yesterday afternoon, Ilse Greenbaum said, "I have seen much and heard a lot and I have begun to understand that it is possible to be happy in Passau. I look forward to going home. But I am taking with me part of my childhood memories from the town I was born in." Today Ilse Greenbaum was driven to the Munich airport where she is scheduled to depart for New York.

From that point on there were no more problems when it came to inviting Jewish emigrants back to Passau as guests of the City. The authorities approved my applications and contributed with relative generosity to the temporary homecoming of the Burian, Blättner, and Hartmann families. The university agreed to make available the reception hall of the central library for an exhibit of Max Hartmann's sketches and Erich Hartmann's photographs. Still, much remained to be done.

Chapter 19

ULRICH ZIMMERMANN IN PASSAU

WHEN RUDOLF RAMELSBERGER, a former classmate of mine and later the legal advisor of the *PNP,* had published the nasty article about me and the two priests, I was not particularly surprised: what else should I have expected from the *PNP?* Anybody who had endured the kind of aggression, resentment, and hatred of the sort that had been directed against me would have known to expect something like this. I put the article down and said to my mother: "No big deal. Just the *PNP* talking again." But my mother felt differently. She was angry and insisted that I should talk to the new editor in chief—perhaps he didn't even have anything to do with it. Perhaps he didn't agree with what had been written? She suggested that I remained polite, yet determined. I didn't feel at all like responding and had no real desire to find answers to these questions, but finally, to satisfy my mother, I gave in: "All right, I won't take it, I'll fight." I wrote and challenged "the new guy" to explain the whole affair to me and to clear it up. I felt that I had done my duty in terms of standing up both to him and for myself, and I gave my mother a copy of my letter. As far as I was concerned, the issue had been taken care of.

However, that was not the case as far as "the new guy" was concerned. A short time later I received an invitation: he had heard a lot about me and would like to meet me. Did I have time to stop by his office and talk about everything?

Truthfully, I was a bit peeved; I thought he had sounded self-serving, hypocritical; a meeting would be silly, a pure formality resulting in nothing. On top of it all, I had a bad cold and didn't feel like seeing anyone. Still, I did show his letter to my mother and asked her opinion. She read it and said, "See, it was worth it after all. Go and talk to him. Whenever people have the opportunity to meet you in person they always come away with a good impression. And maybe he'll be glad to see who you really are."

My mother was right, but at the same time I wasn't overly enthusiastic about meeting a *PNP* person, I must admit: what would "my people" think of me if I told them that I went to meet with a delegate of the *PNP?* That rather than refusing to meet with the editor in chief, I had in fact accepted? But it was this very thought that brought out the unconventional in me; it might be just the sort of challenge I needed. The *PNP* and me. Why not? He might be nice, in spite of being from the *PNP*. And even if he wasn't, it was at least worth a try.

I responded, and told him that I would be willing to meet with him. The secretary said that unfortunately the soonest she could schedule me for was in a few weeks; the editor in chief wanted to be sure that he had sufficient time to spend with me.

By the time our meeting rolled around, my cold had gotten much worse, and I had had to pump myself full of penicillin just to be able to get out of bed that morning. I came back home from the university after class and took more penicillin. My voice was nearly gone. I had a high fever and just wanted to crawl back into bed. I was standing at the bus stop ready to head back home when I thought to myself: if I don't go, he might think I'm chickening out. If I tell him the truth about having lost my voice he might not believe me. And I certainly didn't want him to think that I was a coward. I decided to go to the *PNP*: how long had it been since I'd been there last? How much hostility had I experienced since then? How much disappointment? I arrived at the second-floor offices completely exhausted, but I didn't want them to know how weak I felt. I wasn't made to wait, and was greeted just a few seconds after I had arrived by Michael Westerholz and the new editor in chief. Mr. Westerholz introduced us and left. Here I was, venturing directly into the lion's den. I tried to appear strong and courageous, not too curious, yet interested. (Many years later Zimmermann would remind me, with a smile on his face, of this moment.)

I liked the way he had furnished his office: all white, severe yet light and airy, low-key yet stylish. When he took his seat opposite me and began to compliment me on my eyes I was so furious that I was ready to leave right then. It was probably due to the penicillin that I instead seemed somewhat subdued. Mr. Zimmermann got up and started pacing the room like a panther in a cage. I was checking him out just as much as he was checking me out. We were like enemies who didn't trust each other but still sought out contact. I was curious as to what would happen next.

He had his hands folded behind his back. He suddenly stopped pacing and stood dead still . . . and then looked at me for a long time. Then he said: "I'm Jewish." He was calm, resolute, and succinct. I stared back at him somewhat incredulous. Then he added: "Now I've told you. You should know this. I wanted to tell you so that you'll understand where I'm coming from. And so you'll know that I have nothing against you and that I would never do anything to harm you. In fact, I admire your work."

That afternoon Mr. Zimmermann and I talked for a long time and actually became allies. Professionally we were still at odds: for instance, it was his opinion that a newspaper's only job was to report the facts, to reflect reality. I felt quite differently. I believed that newspapers possessed enormous power and that they should use it in a way that would assist the weaker members of society and help minorities. I thought that a newspaper could and should help steer things that were persistent problems in the right direction, and call attention to deserving issues. I felt it was a newspaper's job to be at the vanguard in helping lead a community into a better future. I didn't see journalists as mere reporters, but as people with the power to change things. Our respective positions did begin to soften somewhat eventually—professionally at least. Privately things were much simpler: we were inseparable for three years. I was fascinated by the world he lived in as a journalist, a world of politics; it was amazing to experience things from his perspective and then to see what the media formally made of it. I enjoyed comparing what he told me in private conversation with what was later reported in his newspaper. Patiently, yet enthusiastically, he repeatedly explained to me why and how certain things were, and were not, being covered. He never tired of reading aloud to me passages he was working on, asking for my input. Whether the subject was world or local politics, human interest stories or satirical pieces, historically significant or trivial matters. We shared our thoughts freely and there was hardly anything we didn't discuss.

I learned a great deal in those three years. This extended look behind the scenes gave me a much better understanding of the many things, not the least of which being the way nuances of language affect meaning and interpretation, which affect the way people think. If anything, Ulrich encouraged me to think against the stream, whether he intended to or not. He taught me to become even more wary of using clichés, to recognize certain gray areas with more clarity and to approach my professional opponents without apprehension. In some cases these techniques actually helped break down many barriers and make possible a certain level of cooperation with people I otherwise would never have cooperated with.

In previous years the *Passauer Neue Presse* had published large advertisements for the ultra right-wing party, the Deutsche Volksunion (DVU), and reported favorably on their activities. This completely changed when Ulrich came on board. The DVU became the subject of great scrutiny. Once one of their major advertisements "accidentally" failed to get printed. After Ulrich Zimmermann came to Passau the *PNP* actually reported extensively on the counter-demonstrations to the DVU, something that had never happened before. Ulrich and I discussed my speech and his editorial. It was a foregone conclusion that in 1987 he and I would together attend a counter-demonstration which publicly spoke out against the DVU. A contingent of hundreds of heavily armed police officers was on the scene (Åke Williams had asked pointedly during the demonstration why the water cannons were aimed at us and not at the aggressive right-wingers). Ulrich was also there in front of the *Nibelungenhalle* when *Bürgermeister* Abelein and I had attempted to gain control of a few dozen anarchists (*Autonomer*), and later when we discussed the measures to be taken against the right-wing extremists the following year.

In 1988 Zimmermann surprised me (and not me alone) with his idea that all political parties, the local labor union, and both the Protestant and Catholic Churches should sign a joint declaration stating: "We do not want the DVU in our city!" The project was dubbed the "Manifesto of the Citizens of Passau." I myself kept a low profile—at least as far as the outside world was concerned—in order not to endanger the entire initiative; it was highly unlikely that the *Oberbürgermeister* would have agreed to sign his name next to mine. But I had made sure that the project would receive excellent publicity. I had called reporters and publicly endorsed the "Citizens' Manifesto"—this had actually confused quite a few people who couldn't understand why I was supporting a project from which I had been so openly excluded. It was not clear to them that, as I have said before, I never really wanted to be an activist, but that I simply wanted to see that the right actions were being taken. It was worth a try, though it would later become clear that for many people their signature was all they were willing to contribute to this cause. One very positive aspect of the project, however, was the continuing successful cooperation of the local press with the cause—at least on this level.

Ulrich and I were quite amused by the expressions on people's faces when they saw us together, especially in the beginning. *He's* working with *her?* Some people took it as a blatant provocation. For us, and for our projects, the relationship worked in very beneficial ways. Eventually what began as a simple lack of understanding turned into open repulsion: How dare you! On the surface our alliance was incomprehensible, our cooperation too unconventional. It was less a problem for me, as a student and a freelance author, than it was for someone in his position. Privately he hardly gave our relationship a second thought. We continued working together, though thereafter more discreetly.

Chapter 20

TUCHOLSKY'S DEATH MASK

GERTRUDE MEYER-PRENZLAU, FROM Hindås, Sweden, was the last partner (*Lebensgefährtin*) and fiancé of the late Kurt Tucholsky, the Berlin-born son of a Jewish businessman persecuted by the Nazis. She had become aware of me and my work in Passau after reading Åke Williams's first article, and had picked up the phone immediately afterward to call him: she wanted the woman about whom he had written to receive Tucholsky's death mask. I should consider it a personal gift from her to me and a symbol of the fact that many people valued and appreciated my work and didn't want me to give up the good fight.

When it had become clear to Tucholsky that he could not prevent the rise of National Socialism, he had expressed extreme sorrow at the fact that not more young people had taken up the fight with him. In 1935 he committed suicide in Hindås. Gertrude found him as he lay dying; there were three letters on his nightstand, one of which was addressed to her. Gertrude read her letter, passed on the other two, and commissioned a friend to make three death masks. One was for Tucholsky's former wife, Mary; one was for his close friend, Walter Hasenclever; and one was for her to keep herself. Mary was grateful to receive the mask, but Hasenclever declined to accept his: "He was afraid I would want him to pay for it," said Gertrude "when in fact it was a simple keepsake." So the mask had stayed with her. "It should belong to somebody Kurt would have loved. To a young person with the courage to stand up for her convictions, someone not afraid to swim against the stream and to let her voice be heard, loud and clear, where she witnesses injustice: 'No!'" Gertrude did not want to see the mask hanging in a museum where people might look at it with interest but, ultimately, indifference. She wanted to be in the possession of a person with whom Tucholsky would have felt at ease. "I have been reading the newspapers and books ever since his death looking for just such a person, but I had never found anybody that fit the description," she said. Fifty years after Tucholsky's death she had bequeathed her mask to the Berlin House of Literature and deposited the third one at the Berlin Senate, only because she had been afraid she might die without ever finding the right person.

Gertrude Meyer-Prenzlau told this story to Åke Williams and asked him to get in touch with me. She wanted me to know that this was not some kind of tasteless prank, but that she truly believed that I was just the kind of person Tucholsky would have loved, would have felt at ease with.

Åke called me right away and told me about her. She was the same age as my grandmother and very strong-willed and determined. "She's a difficult woman who knows what she wants," he said, "but she also always does what she says she will do." He told me she would call me and tell me about her plan herself. I was stunned. And I didn't have much time to really think about what I had just heard; I had just hung up with Åke when the phone rang again; it was Gertrude. "This is Gertrude," she said, "but you can call me Tospy; that's what Tucholsky used to call me. Have you heard of Tucholsky? Have you read anything of his? I want you to have the mask. He had always looked for someone just like you, unfortunately in vain. He would have loved you." I couldn't quite grasp what was happening. She definitely sounded determined, but she also sounded very kind. She spoke flawless German, with no trace of an accent, and finally added: "When do you want to pick it up? It's in Berlin. Or should I have it sent to you by mail?" Considering the problems I'd had with the postal system . . . and given the possibility that the mask could be damaged in transport? No, I told her, I would be happy to come to Berlin to pick it up in person.

My mother was just as surprised as I was. She suggested I not tell anybody about it until everything was confirmed in writing. Who knows? she argued. Someone might intervene in the meantime or Topsy might even die. I didn't say anything about it for a few months. Apart from Åke and Felix Kuballa, there was only one journalist I really trusted: Rolf Henkel of the *Münchner Abendzeitung*. I decided to tell him about it.

His report appeared in several papers, among them the *Abendzeitung* itself, on page three. The headline read: "A Prize for Stirring around in the 'Brown' Swamp."

Henkel wrote in the style that had become his trademark:

The young woman speaks with barely a trace of anger: "The atmosphere here in Passau," she says in her sympathetic, soft voice, "is very tense; things are ready to explode." Since the once well behaved young student from a good middle-class, Catholic household revealed how a couple of pious Passau clergymen had once dealt with Jews, she is known as a troublemaker in her hometown. In other places she is admired for her courage. Today she will receive Tucholsky's death mask in Berlin—as "an acknowledgment of her fight against neo-fascism," in the words of Tucholsky's former *Lebensgefährtin*, Gertrude Meyer-Prenzlau.

Passau, the episcopal town where the church bells frequently chime . . . in the city where Hitler once . . . lived . . . as a boy, . . . in which the murderer of Jews, Adolf Eichmann, was married with great pomp, and where today the DVU, the extreme right-wing party, lives out its pan-Germanic fantasies every summer at its annual convention . . . this is a town where the most recent history has not left its most flattering mark.

Henkel then went over my whole story, one more time, and ended with a quote from Tucholsky: "There is nothing more difficult and nothing that demands more strength of character than to live in full opposition to one's own times and to say loud and clear: No!"

Heiner Lichtenstein wrote in the *Tribüne*:

Everyone knows Kurt Tucholsky . . . his death mask is the most valued possession of his former *Lebensgefährtin*, Gertrude Meyer-Prenzlau. The ninety-year-old Meyer-Prenzlau, who lives in the vicinity of Göteborg, has now parted with this memento and given it to a young German woman—out of admiration. "If Tucholsky were alive today he would enjoy Anna very much," says Ms. Meyer-Prenzlau. The gift is more than a gesture. Its purpose is to encourage Anna Rosmus to continue her work and to serve as a slap in the face of those who try to defile her name. The now famous quote by Tucholsky was true in his time and still is true today. Germany has more than its fair share of conformists and people who run with the pack. To swim against the stream has always required much more strength than simply "going with the flow." Tucholsky's mask will be in good hands with Anna Rosmus—better than if it were to hang in a museum where people might look at it with interest but fail to get its message, much less to live their lives by it . . . despite the many occasions even today, and not only in Bavaria, which call for someone to say stand up and say "No!"

This time even the *PNP* reported in length on the event. Michael Wester-holz stopped by my home and later wrote:

The phone is ringing off the hook at Ms. Rosmus's home, and visitors from all over Europe are coming to see her. . . . Reporters from television and radio stations, newspapers and magazines are asking to meet her. They want to find out what's behind what on Swedish television is being called "the Rosmus Phenomenon": a young woman who does her most amazing work when the pressure is greatest.

Owing to yet another death threat, I never went anywhere in Berlin by myself. Åke Williams had made a special trip from Sweden to accompany me to Berlin where I was to receive the mask. He reported on the occasion for the *Göteborgs Posten*. Together we visited the recently opened exhibit on the grounds of the former Gestapo headquarters, we went to a meeting at the Jewish Community Center, and generally just strolled around Berlin—remaining safe. On May 7th the day finally arrived and I was given the mask during a ceremony at the Tucholsky Museum.

I was surrounded by reporters who were all pushing their way forward to get interviews with me. Åke whisked me away to the Journalists club, where many of his colleagues were already waiting. We had barely arrived when I received a call from Michael Westerholz, asking for a few statements he needed for yet another article for the *PNP*. After this latest article had been published in the *PNP*, Åke Williams wrote a furious letter to the editor:

For almost an entire week the German press has been grazing on old news; news that has long been known to the foreign press and that made its way through the rest of the world a long time ago; in Germany in the meantime, the media periodically "lowed" its indignation before dozing off into a pastoral silence. A foreign observer such as I might be excused for expressing his amazement at this state of affairs.

The headlines were grandiose, and the various reports bordered on the melodramatic:

Anna Rosmus, the twenty-seven-year-old academic and mother of two children, who has been exposed to years of persecution and terror, on whom had been loosed the Pope's Bull and the gamut of small-town vitriol, and who has been the general object of slander because she dared to research the past, has now become an international celebrity in this small and pious town in southern Bavaria.

"Revealing reports in the foreign press about scandalous events in Passau have unexpected consequences," read the major German newspapers: There were official greetings from the Israeli president, inquiries to and from the office of the *Bundespräsident*, expressions of sympathy from all over the world, interviews with the international press and more reports in West German, American, and Swedish television. The crowning glory was a great symbolic gift from Sweden: the death mask of Kurt Tucholsky, the eminent German writer and critic of the Nazi regime who was persecuted by the Nazis and whose books were burned by Hitler's henchmen. The mask was given to Anna Rosmus by the ninety-year-old Gertrude Prenzlau—in honor of her moral courage.

In the wake of all this international attention the German press realized the embarrassing mistake it had made in having closed its eyes for years to a scandal that not only tainted the image of Passau, but the image of Germany as a whole. Suddenly everyone is in a mad rush to do a complete about-face. Suddenly the dauntless young student who dared to research honestly and objectively the past of her home town— a town that to all outward appearances would seem so pious and a past that had been swept so neatly under the rug—is no longer known by the moniker "Anna Horseshit" (*Roßmist*—a pun in German on the resemblance between "Rosmus" and "Rossmist"), no longer is she seen as the one who dirtied her own nest (*Nestbeschmutzerin*); rather she is now renowned and widely discussed. The dominant local newspaper that once persecuted and harassed Anna Rosmus has now decided to celebrate her as the standard-bearer of the honor of a great city.

It was a deplorable display—at best a nod to a biased readership.

But what this particular local newspaper—and nearly all the other papers as well—chose not to mention was an episode that occurred while this esteemed historical researcher was on her way home from Berlin to Passau. Just outside Nuremberg (!), neo-Nazi terrorists were lying in wait with huge logs that they threw across the train tracks. The day was May 8th, the anniversary of Germany's capitulation to the Allies. Fortunately, the tree trunks were discovered and only a few wagons derailed, resulting in a delay of a few hours.

The usually quick-witted German press also failed to mention the (of course, anonymous) letters Ms. Rosmus raked in upon her return. Among them was an article cut out of the newspaper and filled with handwritten slurs like "stinking Jew-whore" or threats like "we will remember your name when it's our turn again," or "you'd better emigrate to Israel."

To outside eyes, said the untiring historian, it seemed that the atmosphere in Passau remained as harmonious as ever. "But in reality it was simply grotesque," Rosmus said, "for me at least."

When Anna Rosmus received the Geschwister-Scholl Award— the highest honor in Germany to be given for moral courage—both

Catholic newspapers in the Passau area (the *Passauer Bistumsblatt* and the *Liebfrauenbote*) claimed that in this case, arrogance has been mistaken for moral courage, a persecution complex for plain slander.

These were the same powerful gentlemen, belonging to that very church, who were standing there during the Third Reich, raising their right arm in salute to Adolf Hitler. Anna Rosmus dared to remind people of that fact.

For some reason it also does not seem to be of interest to make public what *Oberbürgermeister* Hösl of Passau told the *Bundespräsident* when he inquired about how things were going in terms of the "Anna Rosmus affair" in this small and pious town.

"Everything's A-OK," the *Oberbürgermeister* responded. "Ms. Rosmus is receiving all the necessary support and helpful information to aid her with her research," he reported. And the office of the *Bundespräsident* in Bonn conveniently decided to swallow this story. There is no more discussion about the files.

Even the most filthy lies will be used if it will help to put up a smoke screen, deflect the truth, or sweep unpleasant facts under the carpet, comments Anna Rosmus. "I'm used to it," she says simply. Most people will resort to anything in order to secure their reputation and their position. It is indeed a deplorable demonstration, especially since this situation would seem to present a real opportunity for the country as a whole to show its goodwill and to apologize, instead of entering the stage waving dull daggers belonging to the past.

Yet the readers of the *Passauer Neue Presse* never got to read this letter: instead of printing it, Michael Westerholz wrote back to Åke Williams in Göteborg: If he was so upset about how the local media chose to report about me, then the only alternative for the local media was not to write about me at all. And that was exactly what the *Passauer Neue Presse* was considering at that point.

But that had yet to happen again.

Chapter 21

THE FIFTIETH ANNIVERSARY OF THE
NIGHT OF THE BROKEN GLASS

IN THE SPRING OF 1988 I had begun to collect material about the events of the Night of the Broken Glass in and around Passau. I thought about ways in which the fiftieth anniversary of this crime could be appropriately observed here. I found survivors and eyewitnesses from that night. I wanted the City to plan some sort of event. In fifty years, never once had any of the survivors been invited to speak on this subject. None of the survivors had ever been invited to come to Passau as a guest, and none of them had ever received any kind of compensation for what had been done to them.

The more details I discovered the clearer it became to me that that night had indeed been the official prelude to the Shoah. On that night the Nazis finally showed their ugly face and made crystal clear just what the fate of the Jews was to look like. That night signified the beginning of the end of traditional German Jewry and its assimilation in German society. The 1938 *Kristallnacht* was symbolic of the criminal state that Germany had become. I had no intention of letting this fiftieth anniversary pass without notice. I was determined that my city should experience, in full awareness, the significance of this date. I was elated when my father came home with a declaration from the Bavarian Cultural Ministry that made it mandatory from now on for all schools to teach their students about the era of National Socialism and the persecution of Jews, not only on a general, national scope, but on the specific, local level as well. Appropriate learning materials would have to be made available to all teacher and student libraries. Finally, something had officially been done. And for Passau itself this meant specifically that *my* books would now be used as official class material.

But I was not satisfied yet. I wanted to see the greater public get involved. I wanted people of all ages to take note of this date: this was the night Germany had dishonored itself, when it had lost the right to be trusted as a nation and had ceased to be a civilized country. I wanted Passau to think back to this night and for the official representatives of the city to acknowledge this guilt. I wanted the victims to be remembered and honored. I wanted the survivors to be invited to speak in public and I wanted them to hear a clear message of apology. I wanted—at least symbolically—to try to have a part of what had been done to them undone. And I wanted the City to take the necessary steps to reestablish contact with Passau's Jews. I wanted them to be reintegrated, to take part in the memorial events of this night, and to honor its victims together with the other survivors.

I asked Ernesto Finger from Santiago de Chile if he would come and give a speech. Back then he lived in Vilshofen, in the vicinity of Passau, and had been abducted and taken to the Passau county jail during *Kristallnacht*. From there he had been taken to the concentration camp in Dachau with other Passau Jews; there he was humiliated and tormented for weeks. Ernesto Finger wrote back to say that he was prepared to come. I asked the City of Vilshofen to invite him, but was told that no money was available. Then I asked the City of Passau to do the same, with the same result.

Several times I tried to find out from the Catholic Church and the city administration what exactly had so far been planned for the anniversary. Obviously nothing had been planned. I asked my uncle to help, also without success. In September 1988 I wrote to the City once again:

Dear Dr. Brunner—

At the beginning of September I made repeated attempts to contact you and Mr. Hösl. Ms. Bahle's successor, however, told me all I needed to know: that the City has planned nothing—at this point—to remember *Kristallnacht* and its victims.

For this reason Dr. Friedberger has asked Mr. Hösl in a letter to do something to rectify this state of affairs. However, as we never received an answer I assume that still no plans have been made.

I once again ask explicitly that the City organize an event. We cannot all simply pretend that there were no victims in Passau. Not only were there victims, there are living relatives of these victims. They are waiting for a sign from us assuring them that, at the very least, the dead have not been forgotten. There are people who survived this regime of terror and are hoping not to be overlooked any longer. Dear, honorable, Dr. Brunner: you know as well as I do how gratefully Robert Klein and Ilse Greenbaum accepted the invitations extended to them by the City of Passau. Next week the Burian siblings will arrive. Don't you think that these people will be disappointed if they arrive only to find that nothing has been planned to commemorate this event? (The father of the two Burians alone had ten siblings. They were murdered in the camps—as were their families. Their mother, too, lost her relatives, among them the Zinner family, formerly of Passau).

Now, at a time when the City has made public the "Manifesto of the Citizens of Passau," an event to commemorate *Kristallnacht* would be the logical next step. (The credibility of the city has already been placed in question after it was made known that, at the time of the DVU counter-demonstration, a CSU Municipal Council emergency meeting was called, after Hoft bakery displayed its giant swastika pretzels in the shop window, and after the dismal turnout by the locals at the counter-demonstration). I can well imagine that Passau's reputation would be significantly improved by an official gesture such as this. Can't you?

I would also think it highly regrettable if various organizations decided to come up with their own separate events just because the City has organized nothing itself. (For instance, the Catholic Church and the German Trade Union Federation (DGB) are planning—independently of each other—a celebration at the site of the memorial for the concentration camp in Pocking.)

Shouldn't it be possible for the same committee that was responsible for putting together the Manifesto of the Citizens of Passau to organize this one event? Do we not already have, in the St. Salvator Church, the ideal site for the event? This is the exact site of the old synagogue before the Catholics razed it to the ground. Where the old Jewish school was located and next to it, the Jewish cemetery. Would it perhaps be possible to hold the already planned inter-faith service at this location? (The deanery is planning to hold the service in St. Nikola). Couldn't "our Jews" be invited to the occasion? I was shocked when I heard somebody state: "Oh, we hadn't actually thought about the Jews. . . ." Don't you think that *at least* one group, either the survivors or the victims, of *Kristallnacht* in Passau should be allowed to speak?

—Ernesto Finger was the sole survivor from Passau, or rather Vilshofen, who was personally arrested by M. Moosbauer, thrown in jail, sent to the concentration camps, and is still alive today.

—Ernest Landau hid underneath freight carriages at the train station in Passau and was the only Jew to escape Hitler's henchmen that night. Can you think of anybody who might be more competent to speak about what happened back then? Who could possibly speak more powerfully on such matters? These people should at the very least be invited. I also believe that it is not enough to simply address *Kristallnacht* as such; it is of at least equal importance to address the specific events which took place here in Passau. (These events have been researched in great detail and the results are readily available.) I believe that we owe these former residents of our region at least this public commemoration. I therefore repeat my request that you make possible such an event. Please let me know of your decision. I was recently informed, upon request, by Dr. Herzig that the St. Salvator Church has not be reserved for any other occasion on November 9th, 1988.

After numerous additional requests an event was finally scheduled—yet, of course, à la Passau: each affair was planned independently, one by the City of Passau without the local trade union, one in Pocking without either the City or the union. And, what was most absurd of all, all of this was done entirely without involving or consulting the Jewish community. I was both shocked and furious; I asked how such a thing could possibly have happened. The explanation was quite simple: nobody had thought to invite them. "We forgot," they told me succinctly. I was dumbfounded. At the very last minute an invitation was sent out: but not to Ernesto Finger, who would have very much liked to attend and who had himself been among the victims that night, rather to Ernest Landau. Not surprisingly, he already had a prior commitment, and (relieved) he declined: what he had experienced that night at the train station in Passau still haunted him, even if he himself had managed to escape.

In the end I too was relieved. The entire undertaking would have most likely ended in a major disaster: the City of Passau had chosen the "heroes" cemetery (*Heldenfriedhof*) as the site for the event. This is the very place where countless Schutzstaffel (SS) soldiers and their general, Hassenstein, were buried. Hassenstein was not just any SS general, he was the man who effectively ruled Passau at the end of the war. He had been responsible for, among other things, the mass murder of approximately two thousand Russian prisoners of war, committed only hours before the U.S. liberators marched in.

In order to get the site ready for this "other" purpose, the Office of Cultural Affairs (*Kulturamt*) had erected two large wooden stars of David. To this day I cannot comprehend this decision and the magnitude of its thoughtlessness. It was then that I made the decision to do everything in my power to ensure that one day an appropriate memorial site would be established.

After all, a unanimous decision had been reached by the city council, in the year 1947, that stated clearly and unequivocally that the City would build a memorial dedicated to "the victims of National Socialism," and that this memorial would be located in a central location of the city. This decision, however, was never enacted. In 1981, while researching my first book, I had discovered this document and since then had worked ceaselessly toward the realization of what had been promised.

In 1983, on the fiftieth anniversary of the seizure of power, a few citizens had collected donations and then handed a voucher over to the acting *Bürgermeister* with the words: we are donating this money to the city of Passau to go toward the establishment of the memorial, as the city supposedly has no money to pay for it. We named but one condition: the memorial would have to be located just outside the *Nibelungenhalle*. This building, built by the Nazis and inaugurated on the occasion of a racist and hate-mongering event titled "Against Jews and Political Catholicism," had long been a symbol of the power and sway the National Socialists held in Passau. Later Passau made national headlines because Franz Josef Strauss used to hold his annual Political Ash Wednesday meetings there. And now the city had served for quite some time as the location for the annual convention of the right-wing DVU.

We—that is to say some young people from the trade union, the church, and the city youth programs—believed that this was the perfect place for the memorial to be located. Right there, opposite of the former Brown House (*Braunes Haus*), where the Nazi marches and parades had taken place. The Jewish postwar community requested back in 1946 that the square between the two buildings be renamed: from *Ludwigsplatz* (named after the Bavarian king) to "Square of the Victims of National Socialism" (*Platz der Opfer des Nationalsozialismus*). This name was not approved at the time by the city council. However, the request to build a memorial *was* granted.

In 1983 the City decided to deny even this request: officially for reasons of fire safety. Apparently the fire hydrants would have been made inaccessible in an emergency. We found this ludicrous: the square was not exactly of elfin proportions, and it had offered plenty of room for parades (where up to 30,000 people were in attendance), flowerbeds, billboards, sausage stands, and many other such things. But the city council remained stubborn. The original decision had been made in 1947 and now, in 1990, the memorial was no closer to being built.

I started to think about alternatives. In 1991 I came across a cover story in the *Passauer Neue Presse* which included a large photograph; it was the gravestone of Lydia and Josef Zach, a married couple. The City had dug up their remains and renovated the marble column and was now offering the grave for lease. Lydia Zach, née Aaron, had been the only "pure" Jew (*Volljüdin*) in Passau to survive the Third Reich. Her husband Josef, who was Catholic, was able to save her—several times under rather dramatic circumstances where he literally had to get her back from the Nazis—and return her to conventional life in Passau. The Zachs had been respected business people until Lydia was made an outcast and was arrested.

I was incredulous: how could the City of Passau desecrate their gravesite like that? How could they simply rip out the memorial plaque with their names engraved on it and dig up their bodies? The cemetery administration told me very bluntly it was because nobody was paying rent on the grave any longer. Who on earth should have been paying? All of their relatives had been killed! Lydia had been the only survivor. My rage continued to mount: I immediately sat down to write and submit a request to the cultural committee (*Kulturausschuß*) not to lease out the gravesite but instead to restore it to its previous condition. I requested that the engraved plaque be reconstructed, just as Lydia Zach had originally ordered it. And I requested that this formerly private gravesite should become a memorial dedicated to all the persecuted Jews of Passau and the people who tried to save them. I followed up on my request again and again, and asked journalists to report on the case. It took two full years before the *Kulturamtsleiter* even submitted my request to the cultural committee; it finally was approved in 1993. On November 9th, 1994, the site was officially dedicated. This time no one "forgot" to invite the members of the Jewish Community of Lower Bavaria; its President, Israel Offmann, came, together with a cantor, to commemorate *Kristallnacht* in Passau and to consecrate the grave.

Chapter 22

EXODUS: IN THE SHADOW OF MERCY

IN DECEMBER 1988 MY second book, *Exodus: im Schatten der Gnade* (Exodus: in the shadow of mercy), came out. It was published by the Dorfmeister publishing company. The business manager knew my sister. As a student she had worked part-time as a waitress in one of our local, traditional beer gardens. He had met her there and had asked her if she was my sister, and asked her what I was doing these days. He told her that the publishing house might be interested in reissuing my book *Resistance and Persecution;* the owner's father had continued doing business with Jews throughout the 1930s; he was committed to the topic and personally wanted to contribute in some way to its cause.

We agreed that it would make more sense for the company to publish my new book. It was a history of Jewish families in Passau and vicinity. I had researched materials for three years, read through stacks of files, looked through photo albums, and collected letters from the last sixty years. I had made countless phone calls and collected information from all over the Western world.

Many survivors and relatives of the murdered Jews had helped me in my project. They had willingly cooperated and answered my questions, some of them very private. They had shared with me their memories and experiences, some of which caused them unspeakable pain and which they would not be able to forget until the day they died—memories that, I believe, must never be allowed to be forgotten, because they show how, step by step, fellow human beings can be degraded to second and third class citizens; how people can be violated and stripped of their rights, and how this can result in wounds that will never heal. And because we, the young Germans, not only should, but must learn from such past mistakes.

The more I found out about those former Passau Jews the more I was moved by their history and the more I felt compelled to declare my solidarity with them. I myself had felt the reality of their fear, of what it was like not just to be cast out, but also to be forgotten. I was also able to experience their gratitude; gratitude for listening to them, for not looking the other way, for being compassionate, and for my attempts to understand. I could sense how long they had been waiting for this and how badly it was needed. I wanted to give them as much as I possibly could. Many times I wanted to be able to offer more: it hurt me deeply to see how humiliating and difficult the struggle for restitution was, and how mercilessly they were treated by the bureaucracy in their attempts to receive things like medication to help relieve some of the lingering pain from the injuries they had received at the hands of the Nazis. I witnessed their tears as they told me about how grueling it was to have to forge a new existence—in another part of the world, without knowing the language, without money, without a place to live, and without friends. More than once I stood by helplessly as one of them fainted in the mere attempt of recollection. I often wished I simply had more money so I could help them out of their misery. I regretted being so powerless. I wished I could start a foundation with the goal of helping them. I wished I had more political influence so I could represent their interests better. But these were all empty wishes.

I was nothing more than a private individual (*Privatperson*) and a mother of two small daughters. I had given everything I had to give. I was prepared to research, to collect evidence, and to combine it with their recollections. I would record their stories, as completely and comprehensively as possible. And I would have it published as quickly as I could. I would go into schools and talk with students; I would lecture and read from my books. I would give interviews and encourage others to look for similar evidence in their own towns and cities.

When the manuscript was completed there was already a publisher ready to print the book. I felt very relieved. Now everyone I had talked to —almost—would see that I had kept my promises. When the book came out I asked the German-Israeli Society in Pocking to ensure that all the Jews whose stories were mentioned in the book would receive a complimentary copy. It was not possible for me to privately finance this effort and, besides, I was pretty sure that most of them were at least as glad to receive an official gift as they would have been to have a private one. I wasn't going to "forget" them, that much was certain. Rather in this way they would be officially put back in contact with their former home. I was relieved not to hear a "No!" this time; the books were promptly bought and sent out.

Everything went much more smoothly this time than it had with the first book: since the *PNP* had warmed up to me a bit, and had even written positive things about me and my work, public interest had grown considerably. Of course, now the book would have to be reviewed. And the *Passauer Woche*, the new free paper (*Anzeigenblatt*) that was owned by one of the main shareholders of the *PNP*, had an impressive layout about *Exodus*, which took up the whole title page and another two-page spread in the same issue. My work was discussed with an almost provocative openness.

The boulevard-press of Munich picked up the story after one of the local bookstores had formally released it. The *Süddeutsche Zeitung* and others soon followed suit. The following report by Johannes Molitor of Deggendorf was a typical example of the kind of press I received:

> When you see her for the first time it is hard to guess that this woman with her girlish looks is in fact engaged in a dedicated and combative search for the traces of our historical past, which we have not yet come to terms with. The Community Youth Association invited Anna Rosmus of Passau; the event was very well attended, not only by young people. . . . This should come as no surprise. Her name is known throughout the diocese and her work has been discussed in the national press; she is the one who shocked her city out of its slumber. She was reading from her latest book. . . . For her "courage, her democratic values, and her determination to find the truth through her research" she was honored with the Geschwister-Scholl Award in 1984, and her name now stands beside the names of Hochhuth, Walter Dirks, and Reiner Kunze.
>
> Anna Rosmus affects her audience. She is less interested in the deportation dates of the Jewish citizens than in what their dreams had been the very night before they were carted off in the direction of the extermination camps; she is interested in their thoughts and in the thoughts of the people who lived next door to them. She collects these experiences, which always remain subjective, the fragments of a "historical truth."
>
> During a discussion that lasted nearly two hours, the author freely shared with the audience how she had acquired the reputation of someone who "dirties her own nest," and how she eventually became so highly committed to the struggle against the right-wing extremists of today. She suspects that she has been misunderstood many times and by many people. It is not her aim to expose or intimidate anyone. She simply wants to move things forward to "uncover what happened then and

113

what is still happening today." The former is the job of the historian; a job that has yet to be accomplished in the majority of our towns and cities.

Chapter 23

HONORING SALOMON FORCHHEIMER

THE MORE I HEARD about Salomon Forchhheimer the more I wished to see him publicly honored in Passau: he was one of the people who thought against the stream and someone who was truly ahead of his time. He had also been a great benefactor of the city and at the same time was a person of great personal modesty. And yet he, too, was a victim back then. His family had been harassed and their property seized from them. And yet there is hardly anything in the city to remember him. On December 27th, 1989, I once again wrote a letter to the City:

Herr Oberbürgermeister—

I am certain that you know as well as I do that Salomon Forch-heimer was not only one of the most respected citizens of our town but also—more importantly—one of its most generous.

Nobody ever came to him in vain: Salomon Forchheimer gave significant amounts of money to the city's poor and to the victims of accidents and natural disasters. To his employees he was considered more a father than a boss. This was not typical, particularly during his time, at the turn of the century. Eventually he and his family became the victims of persecution and expropriation. Passau never thanked him for what he did. He has been dead now for many years. I am now asking you to please make an effort to do something for him, in his name and in his memory, as a belated gesture of gratitude. Think of a way in which we all, at least posthumously, can show that we honor him.

My plea, however, fell on deaf ears.

Chapter 24

THE NASTY GIRL

IN JANUARY 1985, DURING a commemorative event for the *Weiße Rose* held in Munich, Senta Berger casually asked me how I was and what I was doing these days. She introduced me to her husband, the movie director Michael Verhoeven, and suggested making a movie based on my experiences. I gave my consent to use my story to come up with a movie that had moral courage (*Zivilcourage*) as its theme and its basis in my life.

I was not actively involved either in the filming or in the writing of the script, and I had almost forgotten about the project when Michael Verhoeven gave me a call in 1989 to tell me that the movie had been completed. He asked if I wanted to see it. Of course I said yes. I was curious to see what he had come up with. I drove to Munich, accompanied by my brother, to see the first cut. There I met Lena Stolze, who portrayed my character, and several other members of the crew. Despite many deviations, the film remained, to my surprise, true to reality. I had not expected to actually recognize "myself," and to find "my" family there on screen. Never in my wildest dreams did I expect that Lena would cry in the very moments that had brought me to tears in my own life. I saw her laugh and triumph at the very moments when I, too, had been overjoyed. I was transported back into my own past! All in the matter of just ninety minutes! About halfway through the film I couldn't take it any longer; I had to leave the room and only returned a long while later. Looking back with such intensity wasn't easy.

Surrounded by the other invited guests, I saw the final cut when the film premiered. With the cameras rolling and the journalists asking their questions, I was barely able to answer. I liked the movie. Even though many details had been made up or otherwise changed, it was still my story, my city, and my family. If it had not been about me, but about someone else instead, I might have loved this film. As it was I simply had endless admiration for the director and the actors for their ability to portray many of my own perspectives.

The original German title of the film was *Das schreckliche Mädchen*, a term which would later become identified with me. The English title, *The Nasty Girl*, brought to mind something in the neighborhood of soft porn. Some people were shocked by the choice, but the American distributor had prepared a plausible explanation, one that I found I could live with: the deceptive title would draw millions of adolescents to the theaters and they would be served up—quite unexpectedly—some political dynamite. I thought this was pretty daring on their part, but the plan seemed to work: the film distributors sold millions of tickets and many people later confessed that they had been fascinated with what they saw, even though they might not have gone to see it if it had not been for this slightly questionable title. The film received several prestigious awards and was even nominated for an Oscar as best foreign film. It received excellent reviews and was shown in South America, Japan, Australia, South Africa, in addition to Europe and the United States.

In Passau, however, it was quite a different matter. There the film met with, primarily, a great silence. The City of Passau even banned public advertising for the movie. The official reason was that the posters showed the naked body of an actress covered in gold body paint, made to resembled a classical Greek statue. Their argument, in turn, met with great amusement: well, if that was the case, then the angels (*Putten*) in the cathedral and all the other baroque and rococo churches shouldn't be displayed in public either! My suggestion was to dress up the little angels in Pampers, to avoid any further offense against public morality. The ads for the film were likewise banned in the Munich subway stations. The owners of movie theaters in Passau were not allowed to place ads in the *Passauer Neue Presse*. Finally, the owner of the local cinema painted a black bikini onto the golden naked figure on the poster. This was the spring of 1990. But after the film was premiered abroad and proved to be a great success worldwide, Passau reacted even more fiercely.

In the *Passauer Woche* of January 24th, 1991, under the headline "More Damage Than Ridicule" Stefan Brandl wrote:

> The mantle of forgetfulness regarding the infamous "1000-Year-Empire" cannot be draped over the "City of the Three Rivers" any longer, thanks to Anna Rosmus. . . . Now Passau has to show what it's made of regarding a topic that may never be put to rest. But how do you explain to a mother in England who no longer wants to send her daughter to Passau as an exchange student because it is swarming with Nazis (see the report in the *Sunday Times*), that what she's seen is a false

image of Passau? And this is but one example. . . . Not only is it the
case that an entire town is being judged and made to look bad, that
prejudices are being rekindled, and personal relationships are being
destroyed here; worst of all: the trust that Passau and all of Germany
have worked for decades to achieve again has been destroyed with one
single blow. Another one of Anna Rosmus's achievements? . . . In Passau, at least, she has ruined her credibility—even if in Hollywood, on
the evening of the Academy Awards, she will receive her applause.

The local section of the paper displayed the following in large bold letters: "Passau Is a Nazi Town!" The article continued:

Strong stuff for the more than three million readers of the largest
British Sunday paper, *The Sunday Times:* in that respected paper *Times*
correspondent Graham Lees (38), in a half-page article, claims that
Passau is a "leftover" Nazi town (*alte Nazi-Stadt*). Its inhabitants are
said to have established a museum in honor of Adolf Hitler, and that
the local bakers bake breads in the shape of swastikas for meetings of
the right-wing extremist party, the Deutsche Volksunion (DVU) held
in the *Nibelungenhalle*. The occasion for this article is the release in
Britain of the film *The Nasty Girl*, a portrait of Anna Rosmus (30) of
Passau and her alleged experiences while researching the Nazi era and
its effects on the "City of the Three Rivers," as well as a recent meeting of the DVU on February 16th.

"I can only refer to statements made by Ms. Rosmus," author
Graham Lees defends himself when questioned by the *Passauer Woche*.
"This film has been acknowledged all across Germany, in addition
to having been nominated for the Oscars and the Golden Globe
Awards and to having received the New York Critics Award of 1990."
. . . Professor Dr. Werner Maser was quoted as follows: "Never, not in
Passau, nor anywhere else during the Third Reich, has a so-called
Hitler Museum been built. He himself had strictly prohibited any such
project."

. . . According to research done by the *Passauer Woche* what is most
likely referred to here is an incident that lies years in the past; on the
occasion of an anti-DVU demonstration, one bakery had its windows
smashed because it was displaying some baked goods that, in the eyes
of the protesters, were shaped like swastikas.

Oberbürgermeister Schmöller concluded his remarks by saying: "It is an
awful thing, the way the City of Passau is being slandered for the whole
world to see."

Chapter 25

SEPP EDER

I WAS HAVING BREAKFAST with my mother one morning when she handed me the paper. Not expecting anything particularly bad I leafed through it. When my mother asked why I had suddenly turned so pale I couldn't answer. Speechless, I showed her an article that said that Sepp Eder had been elected deputy mayor (*dritter Bürgermeister*). Sepp Eder! I read the report again in complete disbelief; it couldn't possibly be true. But I had indeed read correctly. Had we not been plagued by enough disasters already? I thought about Ulrich Zimmermann. How could he have allowed this to be printed without a single bit of commentary? How could he publish an article like this, as if it were the most natural thing in the world?

My mother was still waiting for my response. I could feel her eyes on my face. But how could I explain to her all the things that were running through my mind at that point? Sepp Eder as deputy mayor was nothing short of scandalous. I couldn't just take this lying down, without some form of protest, without shuddering at the very thought, without doing something. I had Sepp Eder's file among my documents. This was the man Johann Fröhler, a former Communist who had worked in the resistance movement against the Nazis and who had risked his life for others, had told me about. I had met Fröhler for the first time years before. He had told me not only about Janik, but also about others who had never been de-Nazified, and about still others who were never brought to justice. About people who were responsible for terrible crimes and who were still living among us, their records having been officially wiped clean. Sepp Eder was one of them.

In January of 1983 Fröhler had shown me a file, a document that detailed the conviction and sentencing of Rosina Bauer. Rosina Bauer was sent either to a concentration camp or to a prison after having been denounced by Eder. She was imprisoned for a long time, until finally being liberated by the Americans. She died just a short time ago. I had read the obituary in the paper; it contained no reference at all to the fact that she had been a victim of the Nazis and that she had been stigmatized through her imprisonment back then—even decades later she was remembered as someone who had been "locked up." Of course nobody remembered why.

Rosina Bauer . . . her name was my cue. Maybe I would be able to find her file quickly. I couldn't really remember any details. But I knew that Johann Fröhler had given me a copy of the ruling against her. And that he had told me that *that* Sepp Eder had been planning to run for the office of mayor (*Bürgermeisteramt*) before. However, this had never come to pass. Johann Fröhler had prevented it, as far as I could remember. Fröhler Senior had told me the entire story with noticeable pride. It is said that Sepp Eder was given a choice: he could withdraw his candidacy, and then everything would remain confidential, or he could carry on with his plans and his file and its contents would become public knowledge. . . . Back then Eder had decided not to run for office. And now, just a few years later, he was brash enough to try again? Both Fröhlers were still alive; why shouldn't Sepp Eder be given the same choice this time? Or was I perhaps misinformed? Was this even the same person? Was the whole thing blown out of proportion?

All I told my mother was: "He can't be mayor. He'll have to go. He will shame us all. He ruined a woman's life, a woman whose son was later killed in the war. Sepp Eder never apologized; as a matter of fact he has done absolutely nothing to indicate that he feels any kind of remorse." I took the paper with me and went to search through my notes.

"Rosina Bauer" had yet to be filed—since I didn't have a secretary, I picked up the phone and called Ulrich Zimmermann to ask him how a report like this could have been published so nonchalantly; after all, this man was not exactly an unknown. Mr. Zimmermann listened to me and then calmly asked if I wasn't perhaps confusing him with someone else; Sepp Eder was a member of the SPD. Perhaps there was another Sepp Eder, somebody else who might share his name, perhaps. I thought that this was highly unlikely. I had seen the ruling and Fröhler had given me such precise details. And he was not someone who was prone to exaggerate.

Ulrich Zimmermann wanted proof. Michael Westerholz drove to the Munich State Archives. He requested the files for Rosina Bauer and copied the contents by hand; it would have taken too long to receive permission to make photocopies, and permission might not even have been granted at all. All doubt was removed. It turned out that Johann Fröhler had been right all along. The next morning the case appeared in the *PNP*. The author of the article was Cornelia Wohlhüter, then-editor of the local section of the paper. Meanwhile the television news-magazine *Stern-TV* had gotten wind of things and called me to ask if I would be willing to accompany them to the Munich Archives and to be filmed by another TV news-magazine, *Explosiv*, while the file in question was being presented to me. Why not? I said. I wanted to see this file anyway. The editor responsible for the story applied for a filming permit—for a TV documentary about me and my work. The permit was issued and the files delivered with a minimum of bureaucracy. The only further stipulation was that the names of third parties (such as judges and secretaries) not be revealed in the footage. I requested copies of the file, as I always did for important cases. I was told that this would take a few days longer and the files would be sent to me. They never arrived, however: due to confidentiality rules. Had they known from the outset that Sepp Eder was alive the files would have never been released to us in the first place. Now they were locked away and not to be released until thirty years after his death.

Nevertheless, the scandal was complete.

On May 11th, 1990, it was reported in the local section of the *Passauer Neue Presse:*

> Accusations against the Mayor of Passau. Just a few days after his election, Sepp Eder has been confronted with a sin committed in his youth, during the Nazi era.
>
> Passau. "An upstanding social democrat," is how he is characterized by his Party colleagues. The longstanding Party Leader (*Fraktionsvorsitzende*) of the Passau city council, Sepp Eder, was elected on Monday in a bipartisan vote with the CSU, to the position of deputy mayor. Now it seems his past is catching up with him: as a fourteen-year-old, back in 1943, Sepp Eder informed the authorities about the remarks of an unskilled laborer who was sentenced to two years in the penitentiary (*Zuchthaus*) as a result. The woman had addressed the young Eder because he was displaying a flag with a swastika on his bicycle, and told him: "I'd be ashamed to have such a flag—with all those innocent people dying." The official police report includes this exchange. The woman was already known to the authorities for making statements that were critical of the Nazi regime. The pesky researcher of Passau's "brown" era, Anna Rosmus, leveled this accusation against Eder: "He has never distanced himself from this action and never publicly

expressed his regret." Rosmus discovered the file approximately ten years ago while doing research for her book *Resistance and Persecution*.

Sepp Eder was "totally surprised" by the accusation: "I racked my brain, but for the life of me I simply cannot remember," he says. When confronted with evidence, however, he modified his statement: "I suppose it must have happened this way, then. And so I can only express my deepest regret. I did not know this woman and I knew nothing about her conviction."

His SPD colleagues in the city council, who informed Eder about the accusations yesterday during a Party meeting, are standing firmly behind their Mayor and suspect that the entire case is politically motivated: "Is it not strange that this issue should come up now, of all times, forty-eight years after the incident took place," said the newly elected SPD *Oberbürgermeister*, Willi Schmöller.

The SPD faction of the city council voted behind closed doors on whether Sepp Eder should remain Mayor. A unanimous vote of "yes" enabled him to stay in office. The grotesque public debate that followed was reflected in the coverage by the *Passauer Neue Presse*.

My uncle became enraged and wrote the following letter to the publisher, which was actually printed by the *PNP*:

> As the uncle of historian Anna Rosmus I had initially planned to stay out of the discussion on this matter. However, as a consequence of a disastrous statement published in the *Passauer Woche* on May 17th, 1990, I feel compelled to speak out. It was stated in an article written by Stefan Brandl:
>
> "The woman who was given the Geschwister-Scholl Award threw the first stone against the SPD man who made a simple mistake as a boy. The fact that now, forty-eight years later, he is confronted with this purely because he's been elected mayor is in our eyes no less a crime."
>
> This statement is particularly harmful because it equates "the duty of a historian" with a deliberately malicious act. Exactly what criteria are being used here? How crazy must a person be to write such a thing? Sepp Eder was no innocent choir boy when he had had the woman committed to prison; he was a mailman-in-training (*Jungpostbote*) and capable of conducting his own business.
>
> Stefan Brandl wrote:
>
> "When Anna Rosmus walks into an archive all of Passau gets nervous." According to this logic we must ask the question: how many undiscovered Nazis and Nazi crimes still exist in Passau?

When Eder denounced the woman I was seventeen years old. There were some old Nazi types in our high school, people who had lost their sense of what was right and wrong through their blind admiration of Hitler. Some of these people hold high-ranking positions today. In 1944 I was among those students taught by the former headmaster by the name of Langmandl. The morning parole (*Morgenspruch*) that had replaced the morning prayer was usually recited by one particular student, who shall remain anonymous. After the "Heil Hitler" was pronounced by the teacher, he would continue the parole: "The Jews are our misfortune." It was simply not true, as some people today claim, that one absolutely had to participate and that each person was individually forced to do so. I want to make it very clear, in the name of my former fellow students, that many of us were not in agreement with Sepp Eder's decision to comply with these new rules.

Another incident, which is barely known in Passau, was the denunciation and slander of Chaplain Martin Ruf. A few fourteen-year-old female students of St. Nikola claimed that the chaplain had made sexual advances toward them. Martin Ruf knew that such an allegation would result in his being sent to the concentration camp. The girls confessed to my brother Hermann, who was just about to be drafted at the time and was still attending high school, that their accusation had been fabricated and that the whole thing was just a lie. The fact that my brother interfered in the affair represented a huge scandal in the eyes of *Oberbürgermeister* Max Moosbauer. He had been trying for a long time to indict the much-hated Martin Ruf. He proceeded to place a request with the headmaster of the school, Nestler, which called for the severe punishment of my brother. Nestler asked for leniency for Hermann, who was getting ready to enter into a military career, but added in his letter to the head district leader (*Oberbereichsleiter*) that Friedberger would be sternly punished, if so ordered.

Anyone who lived through this time knows how difficult a time it was to live in. But at the same time they know that it was still possible not to become a beadle for the Nazis (*Büttel der Nazis*) or an informer. The system back then was based on terror and fear and many learned to adapt to it, but there were also those who refused to be corrupted.

Anna Rosmus does not have a political motive. She is not a member of the CSU or the SPD. Her position is motivated by her conscience, and she has the courage to say what others are afraid to say or don't want to hear. The people of Passau—or rather, a few scribblers and squabblers—should stop screeching because somebody has stepped on their toes; instead they should be grateful that, by means of measured academic research and timely publications, someone is finally dealing with part of the past and showing us the way to a better future. Anybody who has paid any attention to the problems of the GDR knows how dangerous it is to simply cover everything up and to declare piously and full of naïveté: let's not talk about this any more.

I myself wrote an open letter to Sepp Eder on June 2nd, in order to clarify my position in detail:

Dear Mr. Eder—

In 1945 you brought charges against Rosina Bauer, an outspoken opponent of the "brown" regime. This resulted in a seven-hundred-day prison term for this woman. Today you claim that you cannot remember anything about it.

In 1948 the Ministry for Special Tasks (*Ministerium für Sonderaufgaben*) issued a wanted persons list with your name on it. You were questioned at that time regarding this denunciation. Can you not remember this, either?

You now say that you would have liked to get to know this woman. She was alive until 1975; she lived in Passau, alone and impoverished. Her house was right in your neighborhood. Why did you never go to see her even once in thirty years?

Rosina Bauer never received any compensation for her imprisonment. She had to suffer all her life from the reputation of being an "ex-con." She was barely able to earn money. Not many people were interested in employing an "ex-con."

Rosina Bauer had to put her son into foster care because she was unable to earn enough money to support him. This son was then involuntarily sent to Russia for five years. When he returned in 1946 he found out about his mother's humiliation, the denunciation, and the imprisonment. He and his wife slept on the floor of their house for three years because the apartment had been destroyed by bombs. He and his wife still suffer from the fact that they were unable to help Rosina in her time of misery.

Rosina Bauer's son is in very bad health, recently undergoing his fourth bypass surgery, and is no longer able to care for his mother's grave. He, too, continues to suffer. I propose that you, personally, should take care of his mother's grave. Before it is removed. Rosina Bauer is your victim, Mr. Eder.

"Too bad that she didn't live to see this for herself," her daughter-in-law has said to me, barely able to believe that somebody does, in fact, remember Rosina, or that anybody would be moved by her fate today.

In 1945 the city council voted unanimously to build a memorial to the victims of fascism; it was to be located on the *Ludwigsplatz*. To this day it has not been built. Have you forgotten victims such as Rosina Bauer? In 1982 I publically reminded you of her and of the decision regarding the memorial. At the time I was told that the City had no money. We, that is to say a few young people and myself, collected 20,000 DM and were prepared to donate it to the City as a gift. In June 1983 the City publicly refused to accept this gift. Since that time the money has been kept in a savings account. Why did you join the others in saying: "We can't accept it?" Why have you never taken any steps to try to make sure that the money would be used some day? Do you simply want to forget about all of the victims?

In 1985 I reminded the City again of victims like Rosina Bauer and of the plans for the memorial. This time I was told that we already had a soldiers' memorial, and that that was sufficient.

Mr. Eder, have you forgotten that Rosina Bauer was *your* victim, not a victim of war and not a soldier?

In 1987 I reminded the City yet again about plans for a memorial for these victims. Your colleague Gerstl stated on camera that he knew nothing about it. He then publicly promised to make it his concern. You remained silent. I suppose you, Mr. Eder, did not know anything about this matter either? At this point Rosina Bauer was already dead. Have you again forgotten the victim, your victim?

Your father was a member of the SS. Have you forgotten about the deeds of the SS? Have you now forgotten *all* of the victims?

When I asked the City in the years 1980, 1981, 1982, 1983, and 1984 to be given access to files from the Nazi era, you remained silent. You, too, were against it.

Have you forgotten that your Party, the SPD, is known, at least in the rest of the country, to be *in favor* of the making such files accessible? Have you forgotten what can happen if significant information is continually kept from adolescents and adults, if they are not given the chance to form their own opinions? Or do you perhaps want the victims to be forgotten altogether, by everyone else? What more do you want? Do you want absolute public amnesia?

Victims must not be forgotten, Mr. Eder. Especially not by someone who is a leader of his party and a mayor.

When, in 1987, a large counter-demonstration was planned against the right-wing extremist DVU, you refused to participate. You told reporters that your cooperation was "not mandatory." Have you

forgotten this incident? Have you also forgotten about the consequences of the "insulated" (*Alleingang*) policies of the Weimar Republic, which led to the very real "separate hangings" of the disunified
opposition parties at the hands of the eventually victorious Nazis?

In 1987 the city council decided in favor of the creation of a new
temporary position by the labor department initiative to research the
history of the Jews. To this day the position has not been filled. Mr.
Eder, have you forgotten about that decision? Or are you counting on
the forgetfulness of all citizens?

In 1989 *Oberbürgermeister* Hans Hösl placed a wreath, in the
name of the city, at the gravesite of Schrönghamer-Heimdal. Where
were your protestations then, Mr. Eder? Have you forgotten that
Schrönghamer was one of the most notorious agitators against Jews
(*Judenhetzer*)? Can one simply forget such a thing? Or did you just
forget to protest? Do not count on the fact that everyone's memory is
as bad as yours! Victims must not be forgotten.

When Passau's asylum-seekers were given rotten food, when they
were forced to live in conditions unfit for humans, you didn't become
active either. Even the *PNP* reported repeatedly on that incident. Did
you simply forget?

You have been city councilman for twenty-two years, Mr. Eder.
How much have you forgotten during this time alone?

It is bad enough when a private citizen has such gaps in memory,
Mr. Eder. But for a city councilman, it is so much the worse. If the
leader of a political party is a bit forgetful it's perhaps an embarrassment to his fellow party members, but in the case of a mayor it is intol-
erable. A mayor who habitually forgets about the weak, the minorities,
and the victims to the degree and as systematically as you have should
retire immediately. A mayor like that scares me.

I hope for a mayor who does not forget. Somebody who stands up
for the weak. But regardless of my own hopes, it is your express responsibility to protect the city. Instead you are destroying it: an informer has
become mayor, someone who simply forgets issues of great relevance.
Or, in other words, a liar. How about that for a headline!

After Philipp Jenninger had caused grave damage to the Federal
Republic of Germany, he resigned. Why don't you show at least that
much character!

Sincerely,
Anna Rosmus.

My open letter, however, was never mentioned, much less published. Everything remained as it always had been in Passau. Yet, in some way an era was

coming to an end: Ulrich Zimmermann was forced to resign immediately after he had reported about Sepp Eder's miserable denunciation. After that nobody mentioned me and these kinds of topics for quite a while, even though, in my humble opinion, there were more than enough reasons to do so.

Chapter 26

A SPECTACLE OF HYPOCRISY

WITH A LOT OF PATIENCE, and a few tricks, I had managed to arrange an art exhibit in the City Museum back in 1986. On exhibit were paintings by a former Passau Jew, Robert Klein. With even more patience and guile I had somehow managed to convince the former *Oberbürgermeister*, the *Kulturreferent*, and many Passauers to show up at the train station and officially welcome the seventy-eight-year-old émigré.

The gentle, still-suffering man and his internationally successful paintings impressed everyone. When he later sent a series of new drawings to the *Kulturreferent* he received the reply: "I think your work is exceptional not only in terms of its technique but in every other respect as well. . . . I would like to express my great appreciation to you for having made your drawings available." When Christmas 1989 arrived he wished the practicing Jew a peaceful and blessed Christmas and reiterated his desire to reproduce the paintings in a bound volume.

In September 1990 the artist was scheduled to return to Passau for the signing. But at the end of July, when Robert Klein wrote to the *Oberbürgermeister*, the *Oberbürgermeister* had written back saying that he was very much looking forward to the occasion. Still no further arrangements had been made.

On August 18th, 1990, the following article was published in the *Passauer Neue Presse:* "The Jewish émigré and artist Robert Klein, who came to Passau for three days in 1986 as a guest of the *Kulturreferent* Dr. Max Brunner, will be returning to the city in September. He will use the occasion to sign his portfolio . . . which will later be presented as a gift to special guests of the City of Passau." The problem was that the City had decided all this without having consulted the artist himself—who had never given his consent to the plan.

Robert Klein was eighty-two years old by then and had been suffering from heart disease for many years. He had recently had to undergo yet another, extremely painful, cortisone treatment at the hospital. When Dr.

Brunner called him at 5:42 A.M. he was in a deep sleep; the purpose of Dr. Brunner's call was to have the artist give his official approval of the plan. Klein, however, had no idea what he would be agreeing to and so refused.

Three days later the City of Passau informed him in writing that a portfolio was already being put together. The book would be published no sooner that early 1991. The city seemed very put off when Robert Klein told them that this was not the way he wanted things done. When the local newspaper inquired about specifics, the director of the city's legal department, Joseph Gevatter, stated briefly and definitively: "The printing of the portfolios cannot be reversed." The *PNP* quoted him and claimed—incorrectly—that Robert Klein had initially given his consent and was now revoking it.

The artist sent a fax to the *Oberbürgermeister* stressing the fact that the portfolio was a great disappointment to him: "I am certain you will understand that a book would mean much more to me." But nobody was interested in the artist's feelings. The City responded at the end of August that a loose-leaf portfolio was nearly completed and that "one did not want to forego" its publication. Four weeks later, Dr. Brunner advised the cultural committee against publishing the book. At that point the printings had not even been ordered yet. Finances were not the issue here, Mayor Wösner pointed out. The committee decided in favor of printing the loose-leaf portfolio.

Robert Klein felt cheated and asked me to officially represent him in all affairs related to this issue; he himself was too sick and too far away. I immediately contacted the new editor in chief of the *PNP* and asked him to get to the bottom of the odd and, in short, extremely rude behavior exhibited by the City officials. However, my letter was simply forwarded to Dr. Brunner. Immediately thereafter his lawyers sent me a declaration of discontinuance (*Unterlassungserklärung*) and threatened to sue: their client's action had been neither deceitful nor arbitrary. When I presented the lawyers and the press with four years worth of incriminating material against the *Kulturamt*, including entire series of letters, they immediately withdrew their threats. Robert Klein again declared to Dr. Brunner that the book would represent the highpoint of his career, and told him that afterwards he would present the drawings as a gift to the Oberhaus Museum, and even add several more to the collection.

Just in time for Chanukah, Dr. Brunner announced that the entire project had been cancelled: the City would no longer be involved in any capacity. If Klein still wanted to see the portfolio published he should contact a publisher, he said, and added that he was enclosing a sample. After this announcement Helene Klein wrote to Dr. Brunner: "If it was your intention to insult my old, sick husband and to make him suffer even more, I can tell you that you have accomplished your task." The disappointed man wrote me a separate addendum to me, in which he said: "A simple rejection was not enough. No, they had to insult me on top of everything else: a loose-leaf portfolio, stapled at the center; the paintings would be shrunk down to the size of postcards. The thing would look like a miniature bus schedule (*Fahrplanbücherl*). . . . The entire production, including the 1986 exhibit would be made into a spectacle of hypocrisy with a 'brown' backdrop."

On January 1st, 1991, I again asked for the help of Rudolf Kollböck, the new editor in chief of the *PNP*, because what was happening was enormously damaging to everyone involved. Damage that, moreover, would be irreversible.

The bedridden artist asked me to get the paintings out of the *Rathaus* and to keep them with me: the entire affair became increasingly stressful to him and many times he suffered from acute shortness of breath. He now constantly required access to an oxygen tank, especially at night.

Again, I was thinking against the stream. I put myself into Robert Klein's shoes and marched toward the *Rathaus*. Carrying the paintings under my arm I walked into the offices of the *PNP* and asked to speak with Cornelia Wohlhüter. I explained to her in detail the entire history of the project to that point and presented her with detailed information concerning the case, such as letters and affidavits, and asked for her to write an article about it. In my opinion such obvious wrongdoing must be made public. The public had a right to know what was going on in the *Kulturamt* and about the way in which the city's legal department was covering for them. I wanted the people to know exactly how the city had acquired its current bad reputation. I also wanted to keep alive the topic of the Jews and the issue of dealing with the past. And I wanted to inspire solidarity with Robert Klein and his work. This time the story was covered extensively by the paper. Cornelia Wohlhüter commented in an article published on January 15th, 1991, by the *PNP*:

> The unfortunate development of the story involving Robert Klein and his paintings has now become more than just embarrassing. What is at stake here is Passau's past and the question of whether a Jew who was persecuted by the Nazis should be granted the satisfaction of knowing

that his paintings will be printed in his hometown . . . to do so would have reflected well on the City of Passau.

Instead a lack of sensitivity has "led to a situation which is highly confusing" and resulted "in alienating Robert Klein for good."

When Cornelia Wohlhüter asked me what I as planning to do with the paintings I spontaneously told her that I was going to publish a book myself. Robert Klein was going to receive the acknowledgment he deserved. And many people would see just how much culture we Germans had lost as a result of the Jews being labeled an inferior race and being forced to leave Germany. If this hadn't happened, sensitive, brilliant artists such as Robert Klein would have been living *here*.

The book was published in December 1991, in both English and German. In order to help finance the project I had asked the *Kulturamt* for a grant of 5,000 DM. The request was finally approved due to the support of three of the councilmen: the City committed itself to purchasing books in the sum of 5,000 DM. They would be given as presents to official guests of the city.

Chapter 27

IS PASSAU A CITY OF CULTURE?

PASSAU CONTINUED TO BE discussed in the media for quite some time. On August 31st, 1990, the *PNP* printed the following headline:

> Passauers are literally rising to the occasion for a competition organized by ZDF. On Wednesday at 7 A.M. a hot air balloon carrying a camera team from Mainz is scheduled to take off into the skies—provided the weather is sunny. The goal is to film views of the city and to show it in its best light from high above.
>
> Filming for the nine-minute tape will last four days. The clip is intended to serve as Passau's introduction to the "Tournament of Cities" (*Städteturnier*) which will take place in Berlin on March 10th. After weeks of preliminary planning, the organizer Stefan Weber came up with a concept for the topic: "What is the Role of Culture in Passau." Four citizens, representing a cross section of the city, were to be asked this question and to present their favorite cultural activities in such a way as to make the city look good. . . . Lots of material for a short, nine-minute slot. . . . The script . . . may turn out to be too long. . . . The final cut is going to be approved by the *Kulturreferent* Dr. Max Brunner. . . . In the meantime, difficulties in booking representatives to appear in the forty minute cultural trailer have arisen. In a letter to the *PNP* . . . the cabaret artist Sigi Zimmerschied declined to participate; and at the moment it looks as though Elmar Raida will not be available either.

Once again the *PNP* reflected the split within the city, the hostility with which individuals attacked each other; even as a stranger one could easily detect how deeply entrenched the fronts had truly become. However, something that was never made public was the plan for a practical joke that was never realized. Originally I was to fly to Berlin and make a surprise appearance, confronting the puzzled *Oberbürgermeister* of Passau by asking him some of my questions on live TV. The idea was tempting, and I could have easily made a fool of him, but all in all it wouldn't have accomplished anything as far as furthering my work went. "You always have to swim against the stream" (*"Du und dein Querkopf"*), I was told when I mentioned the idea to people I knew. And I respected their opinion: But I no more wanted to be used by the City of Passau for their cheap purposes of self-promotion than I wanted to serve as a spokesperson against the city. So I stayed home.

Passau, with its own cheap gags, would become the subject of enough ridicule without my help.

Chapter 28

POLAND 1991

MY DAUGHTER SALOME HAD since turned six and was now in the second grade. The two foreign girls in her class were her best friends. She frequently brought Claudia to our house after school and they did their homework together; afterwards they played and Claudia frequently stayed to spend the night. One day her father came by and told me that he was very worried: Claudia was ashamed to tell people that she was Polish, to speak Polish at home, and even to go to Poland with her family for summer vacation. He wanted her to be able to speak both languages, or at least to continue returning to Poland for visits. He told me that he had tried everything but she now insisted on staying here with Salome. I felt sorry for the girl; I had grown to like her very much. Ever since her family moved to Passau she and Salome had become close friends. The girls were four years old at the time. But I also understood that it was important for Claudia not to forget her roots and her origins.

Before I could make a suggestion, her father asked me whether Salome might be allowed to go with them to Poland for three weeks. He, his wife, and their three children would be leaving in about ten days. Claudia was only willing to go if Salome came along.

Salome was excited; of course she would come! Claudia and her and a trip to Poland. Still, there were a few practical questions to be resolved: four small children in one car, the oldest just having turned seven, the youngest barely two? Salome couldn't speak one word of Polish. Salome suggested they stay for ten days instead. She was not afraid—but three weeks? On the other hand, it would hardly be worth taking such a long journey to stay only ten days.

Claudia's father then tactfully suggested that I might want to come with them, with both my children. I had, in fact, wanted to see Poland for a long time. And so it was settled: a week later the school holidays began; we packed some essential clothes, photo equipment, and some food and we were off. Bogdan, his wife Danuta, and their two smallest children would take one car, and I would follow with Claudia and my own two daughters in another. We took some shortcuts, known only to locals, which took us straight though the Czech Republic. My command of Czech was miserable, and I was relieved that Bogdan could count it among his impressive repertoire of languages. Claudia was very quiet during the entire trip, which was not typical of her; she was usually a very lively child. We hadn't even gotten to Poland when she told me that she was already looking forward to going back home, because her home was in Germany now.

My command of Polish basically consisted of a few polite phrases and questions—enough to get me by in an emergency. When the customs official asked us for our passports I was just barely able to understand him. When he wanted to know where we were going and whether we had anything to declare, I was lost. At that moment Claudia jumped in, ready to help. She translated my phrases into Polish for the customs officer, and then back again, from Polish into German, for me. The little girl amused him. From that moment on, Claudia clearly felt more at home. She spoke Polish more or less fluently; she reserved our hotel rooms for us, arranged for a researcher's room (*Forscherzimmer*) in museums, and inquired about the opening hours for Holocaust memorials. And last but not least she helped us read the menus in restaurants.

Bogdan saw a changed and happy daughter. She was quite obviously proud of herself. She showed us her home country and my daughters got to know Poland—not from the typical perspective of the tourist from the West, but from the point of view of a Polish girl. We were invited to visit her grandparents, we grilled out with friends of the family, we petted their cats and climbed their trees and also, together, we visited the memorial site of the former concentration camp in Auschwitz.

We stayed the night with their relatives in the country and slept on the straw in their barn. Chickens were perched on their roosts above and beside us, and in the morning the children learned first hand what it meant to "slop" the hogs. There was no running water and no way to take a bath. When we arrived they slaughtered a pig and prepared sausages from the meat for us. What remained of the carcass was taken to town the next day by two men in a horse drawn wagon and sold there. In the evening the adults went to the local pub—where I was supposed to get a taste of true Polish life: how they lived, thought, and talked. My Polish began to improve slightly, due in no small part to the many older people who could speak German and were able to explain to me what was being said. During the time of the Nazi occupation they had been forbidden to use their own language and were forced instead to communicate in German.

I was sitting with them and everybody could recognize that I was from Germany. I frequently felt ashamed for what had been done to those people in the name of my country, and I often thought how directly responsible we Germans were for their poverty, for what had been destroyed there by the war and never been rebuilt. I saw their old, worn hands and their scars, the traces of suffering in their faces, and I thought over and over again: Who did this to you? I wanted so much to apologize and to make good what others had done before me but of course that was impossible. I didn't have the language skills; but even if I had, no words would have been adequate.

I thought of the farce of the so-called restitution (*Wiedergutmachung*). Even those lucky enough to get back anything at all were receiving next to nothing. German Jews were officially entitled to receive restitution payments, but the amounts, if they were granted at all, were very small indeed. And here in Poland hardly anyone had been officially approved as a recipient. I am almost certain that none of the people I'd met had ever been given a penny.

Everybody there knew that I was German, but I never experienced any kind of disdain. People were very hospitable and seemed to be genuinely interested in us young Germans. Poland made an indelible impression on my children as well: on the one hand it was pure adventure, full of novelty and risk; on the other they were aware of the openness with which people everywhere treated us foreigners. In the streets where nobody knew us, at the memorials of concentration camps, where my books and essays were on display and piles of newspaper articles about me had been hoarded, at the Russian border and at the farmers' market in Warsaw. Most of the time we were accommodated in museums; it is the custom in Poland that museums provide rooms for researchers. This was a fascinating experience for the children, as was the fact that again and again we saw horse-drawn carriages on major highways.

I was pleased to see that both of my daughters responded with empathy, and not arrogance, to the poverty they witnessed. I was relieved that they didn't reject these new experiences, but that they were curious to see and to learn instead. Both of them picked up a few words and phrases of Polish, just enough not to seem impolite. They both patiently trudged along beside me when we visited the concentration camps. They even discussed why they found Treblinka the more impressive and Auschwitz the most significant.

They had loved certain parts of the Italian coast where they used to spend their summer vacations with my parents, but they were fascinated by Poland. I was already looking forward to the next trip to Poland: Dzamila Ankievitz intended to create a documentary film about the child murders in the Passau region; it would be based on material I would publish in my book *Wintergreen—Suppressed Murders*, a work which would create a year-long, worldwide stir.

Chapter 29

WINTERGREEN—SUPPRESSED MURDERS

BASED PRIMARILY ON MATERIALS held at the National Archives in Washington D.C., in 1993 I was able to come up with a relatively complete portrait of the concentration sub-camps (*KZ-Außenlager*) Pocking and Plattling. I also documented the murders of approximately two thousand Russian POWs as well as close to one thousand children of foreign descent in the Passau area. All four of these chapters in history were relatively unknown until then. And all this had taken place close to the end of the war in the vicinity of my hometown; one crime more repulsive than the previous one and each in blatant violation of existing human rights laws. Not one of these crimes had ever been acknowledged or atoned for. They weren't even documented. I felt a huge sense of shame and was determined not to accept the collective silence (*allgemeine Schweigen*) one minute longer. I was sick and tired of the fact that there was quite obviously no sense of guilt about any of this and that daily life was still conducted as though nothing had ever happened. Some of the perpetrators were still walking the streets freely. While the few surviving victims were still suffering as a result of persecution.

I had first heard about Dr. Franz Maria Clarenz back in 1980 when I wrote the essay for the student competition about the prewar years; after the war he became known to American readers as the "Herod of Hutthurm." This was the first time I read about the forced abortions that were performed at his clinic which had caused the town to be known as "the slaughterhouse." I also knew that the priest Ludwig Winkler, who had tried in vain to stop the procedures, had been shot and killed. But I had not been able to find out any more details.

Things changed, however, at the end of 1992, when I got access to the files at the National Archives in Washington. Thereafter I was able to write the first chapter for *Wintergreen—Suppressed Murders*. In yet another chapter I published photographs, documents, and eyewitness accounts concerning the concentration sub-camp Plattling, which was located only a few miles from Passau and where hundreds of people were killed. The memorial, which had been erected at the site immediately after the end of the war by the few survivors, was torn down in the 1950s. The building materials had been "recycled" to construct new gravestones and to pave a street.

My section on the massacre of the Russian prisoners of war received a great deal of attention: not only were these crimes committed literally during the final hours of the war, but they also were carried out with extreme brutality. And not a single one of the perpetrators was made to stand trial for the atrocities. For me personally the fact that Ludwig Rankl had been involved was especially shocking. A Russian who himself had barely escaped had stated under oath before the American investigators that Ludwig Rankl, while still in uniform, had seen to it that his Russian comrades would not survive despite an initially successful attempt to escape. Had he not found the escapees and betrayed their hiding place they most likely would have survived. But they were found, with his help, and shot just hours later. Ludwig Rankl to this day is incumbent mayor of our neighboring community of Tiefenbach.

In 1980 I had come across several old newspaper articles which indicated the existence of a concentration camp in Pocking as well as the existence of a small Jewish postwar community there. I knew that the rabbi was named Lipot Meisels and could sense that he had been a fascinating man: he had spent years in the concentration camps and had survived to later build a potent (*gewaltig*) monument following the war in memory of those murdered. No one was able, or willing, to tell me whether he was still alive or not and, if so, where I might find him. I had been searching for him for twelve years: wherever I gave a talk, whether in Hamburg or in Houston, in New York or in Göteborg—I always made a point of inquiring about him. For twelve years I had asked without receiving any answers.

One day in Houston, after a fund-raising event for the planned Holocaust center there, I was told by one of the former occupying soldiers that, yes, of course he knew Meisels. He said that Meisels was living in Jerusalem and that his oldest daughter was living in Dallas. I called her immediately and was overcome with emotion when she said that her father was in good health and as active as ever, that she just was about to go visit him: for years he had refused to talk about those years but she would speak on my behalf. I wrote a letter to the rabbi and asked him to read my completed chapter about Pocking and to possibly suggest corrections or improvements; I also asked him if he could provide me with additional photographs or documents. The rabbi answered in German and assured me of his full support. In addition, he offered hundreds of documents for me to see. He was happy that there was finally somebody who showed an interest in the matter—and, of all people, a German. He had walked to the mailbox to send off the letter himself—and died on his way home.

Before I even received the letter, the former occupying soldier and liberator called and told me what had happened. I was as grief-stricken at the news of his death as I had been happy on the day that I had received his address. I felt guilty as never before: he had been happy and full of life—until he received my letter. Now he was dead, all of a sudden and without warning. I didn't know how to behave toward his children, what to say, how to apologize.

A few days later his daughter Mirjam called me from Dallas. She had found a draft of a letter her father had written which made it clear to her that her father's last wish was that I receive the documents. She had discussed this with her siblings and they all had agreed to respect his wish. None of them spoke any German or French, and thus were not able to read what he had written, or to tell which of the documents would be useful or relevant to me. So they asked me to come to Jerusalem and to view the documents with them. She assured me that whatever I needed I could have.

I met Rabbi Meisels' children as soon as I arrived in Jerusalem. Mirjam looked very American, she was blonde and spoke both English and Hungarian, her native language. Her younger sister, Judith, a very beautiful woman with dark hair, spoke English and a little Hungarian. The older brother, Simon, was slim and wore a uniform. He was working for the security service for the State of Israel and was very helpful to me in filling in the gaps in the documents by recalling stories and memories of his mother. The youngest son, Daniel, was an orthodox rabbi. For that reason he was not allowed to shake my hand, but he readily translated for me a series of religious documents, which had been written in Pocking, from the Hebrew. He explained the obscure rules that had existed at that time and what made the documents unique. His knowledge was tremendously helpful to me.

We spent days just sitting together looking at photographs and identifying documents, each person taking turns to translate what they found. What we learned was as interesting for me as if was for them. Again and again they reassured me that their father's death was not my fault, even though they were convinced that he would not have died so abruptly were it not for my letter. I guessed that my questions might have burdened him so much that they had simply caused him too much agitation and stress. They saw it differently: they thought that their father was unable to die all those years because he didn't yet know who would care for his memorial and who would write it all down. As soon as he had received my letter he called all four of his children and asked them to come to see him. He had told them things he had never been able to talk about before. They all agreed that only then had he felt free to die. This sounded strange to me at first, but the more I heard about him the better I was able to understand.

They gave me everything I asked for and I decided finally that a museum should be built in Pocking. A museum that would tell the story of this rabbi and the history of the Pocking concentration camp. It should be a museum that would show the blossoming Jewish community this man had helped to build in only three years and would reveal the circumstances of its merciless and brutal end. I was determined to see that the memorial, which Meisels had built with tremendous difficulty, would be restored to look exactly like it did when Meisels had had to leave it behind in 1949. I would make it known that the Bavarian Castles and Lakes Administration (*Schlösser- und Seenverwaltung*), who had removed all the names of the murdered inmates, would keep talking and writing about this until the Stars of David and the crosses were restored on the stone tablets just as Meisels had had them engraved there.

I had no illusions about how difficult such a project would be and how long it would take to be realized. A chapter in my new book was just the beginning. The book was already making waves six months before it was to be published. It brought dozens of camera teams to Passau and to Pocking and I made sure that they all got a shot of the memorial that had been desecrated by the State. Rabbi Meisels' memorial would become a symbol of how we Germans were dealing with our past today. It became a place of mourning and a place of remembrance far beyond the borders of Europe. Far beyond Rabbi Meisels' wildest dreams.

The Free State of Bavaria (*Freistaat Bayern*) had continually refused to restore it, and I was considering whether I should do it myself—with the help of the few survivors of the concentration camp Pocking and in the presence of American liberators from back then. As an individual I had no right to do so, but I felt that as a German it was my duty.

Chapter 30

USA 1994

IN THE SPRING OF 1994 I returned to the United States for a few weeks to help raise money for the Anne Frank Foundation to finance exhibits. My primary task was to talk about my research on Passau and the National Socialists, but I was also asked to relate my personal experiences in trying to do so, about being stonewalled, and about the reluctance of the authorities to assist me. At the end of these speeches I was supposed to answer questions from the audience. One of the things I was asked almost every time was how to deal with such an attitude and what could be done to help people like me. I always gave the same answer: "Help me to find survivors from Passau and help me to find the liberators. Help to ensure that discrimination will not be tolerated in your own hometown and help us fund the Anne Frank exhibit." Fund-raising requests were sent out, information sheets were distributed, and there were many volunteers to help out with all aspects of the event. It was a good feeling to be part of this and to help educate and sensitize people.

It was also very good to be accepted by so many people as one of them. On my thirty-fourth birthday I found myself—yet again—in Texas. A group of lawyers put me up at one of the classy, company-owned apartment suites downtown. I was taken out to a concert, and one of the lawyers even organized a surprise party for me in a traditional Mexican restaurant. All the guests got Texas cowboy hats and the waiters sang "Happy Birthday" to me. We celebrated late into the night.

A few days later I was in California, where Bruce Babitt was speaking in Santa Cruz about protecting the Bay. It was a very mixed audience, with people carrying babies, grandfathers and grandmothers, hippies with posters displaying slogans, and school children dressed up in their best clothes. The mayor of Santa Cruz announced the establishment of an "Anna Rosmus Day," and a congressman by the name of Darling invited me to stay for a week at his inn. It had a view of the coast and I could see seals and fishermen and the joggers (for whom a guide had been organized to regulate traffic, as the congressman explained). Amused, I took it all in; I appeared at the press conference and patiently endured yet another party filled with people who wanted to congratulate me. There were altogether six mayors present. I rushed from one event to the next, gave lectures at universities, and attended benefit events and official dinners with the "important" people.

While traveling I worked on my book and interviewed survivors from the Passau region. I pieced together various information that I had collected in archives and continued my search for the liberators. The Dutchman Barry van Driel drove me up the California coast to show me the hundreds of elephant seals. Bruce Giuliano, whose parents were from Italy, took me to San Diego and showed me the world-famous wildlife park where thousands of animals could roam free instead of being pinned up in cages—and where tourists could approach only in small groups so as not to disturb them. I was fascinated by all of this; it was so different from everything at home.

In the meantime, though, I became more and more preoccupied with the idea of how wonderful it would be if the survivors of our former concentration camps and the liberators could be able to meet again, now, fifty years later. This time they would not be skeletons at the brink of death and men in uniform, but they would all come as guests of the municipality (*Landkreis*). I thought about the kind of impression it would make on the young people of my hometown if they were given the chance to hear about them and their stories first hand. I thought about how the victims would feel to know that they were not simply forgotten or disregarded. And I thought how good it would be if the mayors of Passau and of Pocking were to proclaim a "Day of the Victims and their Liberators" (*Tag der Opfer und Retter*).

But I had lived in Passau too long to be so naive as to think that this task would be easily accomplished; I knew that I would have to fight for it, that there would be hardly any volunteers, and that I'd have to do most everything myself: I'd have to find the people, formally invite them, motivate my people in Passau, convince the media to get involved, do all the fund-raising, and come up with a set program. I also knew that I was quickly running out of time. Most of the prospective guests were now in their early eighties. Many of them wouldn't live much longer. I had to act fast. I made use of every single piece of information and every single interview in order to draw attention to this project.

Privately, there was yet another idea going through my mind, especially late at night. I kept thinking of Shelly Shapiro, who had been asking me for the last two years whether I might like to move to the United States. I thought about the rabbi in Albany who had invited my children to attend a Jewish summer camp and who had offered to help me with all the arrangements. He had even offered to supply a rent-free apartment so I could continue to work on my dissertation without having to worry about money. I thought about Elie Wiesel, who had asked me back in 1990 if I wanted to move to Boston to complete my studies. The question of my moving and continuing my work in the U.S. came up again and again.

After three and a half years I was finally ready to seriously consider such a step: my older daughter had just turned twelve; she had been studying French for two years and was now getting ready to start learning English. She was enthusiastic about the idea of moving. My younger daughter was nine and had almost completed elementary school, so she would probably be switching schools anyway. I was only months away from completing my master's degree. My divorce was final—ten years after it began the marriage had failed. I had foregone accepting any alimony in order to be free. I was ready to start looking for a job and earning my own money. Passau offered me no realistic perspectives—not for the kind of work I was doing. So I was going to end up moving, with my children and my dog, one way or another. The only place I was considering in Germany was Berlin. I had loved that city ever since I first visited it at the age of sixteen, when my father had taken me and my mother with him to attend a political seminar organized by the Hanns-Seidel-Foundation, a conservative political foundation with close ties to the CSU. The perspective of the lecturers was strange; afterwards I had the feeling that everything in life was somehow related to the attack that the "other" Germans were planning. But the topic of "East versus West Germany" (*Ost/West*) was still fascinating. For the first time in my life I ate Turkish food, with Turkish people. I saw shops that stayed open all night and a diversity in the streets that I had never seen before: people of various skin colors, speaking different languages, wearing different clothes, and coming from a multitude of cultures. I liked the modern architecture of the *Maria Regina Martyrum*, the Catholic memorial church dedicated to the victims of suppression in the Nazi era; I was impressed by the place of execution (*Hinrichtungsstätte*) in Plötzensee. Of course I didn't know then that our Priest Mitterer had been executed there because he had repeatedly taken a stand against the Nazi regime. I could live in Berlin, I thought.

On the other hand, America was at least equally as tempting: even more cultures, with even more of a mix of languages, were represented there than in Berlin. Most of the archives I had been using for years and which were critical for the continuation of my work were in the States. So many of those who had offered me their support were living in America. Professionally there were any number of interesting paths I could follow. My children would learn English and have the chance to grow up in a multicultural society. They'd be able to experience for themselves what it meant to be considered a foreigner (*Ausländer*). They would see what it meant to be new to a place and not to be able to understand many things; they would learn to see things differently.

But I had to be careful, I didn't want to ask too much of them. First of all we'd have to find a neighborhood where we would be neither the only white people nor the only foreigners, in order not to become isolated. It should be a place with a good mix of people. And the area would have to be safe: each day in the U.S. some fourteen children were killed by guns—this is not even counting the ones who went missing or the ones who survived the gunshots. And not counting the ones who were killed in street fights or died of drug-related causes. I wanted my children to learn not how to die, but how to *live*. I wanted them to learn not how to hate, but how to *love*. I wanted them to grow up in an environment of sympathy, not aggression. I wanted them to live in freedom, not fear.

I wanted them to attend good schools in a safe neighborhood. I visited approximately sixty schools, mostly in the Boston and Washington D.C. areas, to make sure that there would be as much diversity as possible and also that the area was safe. Silver Spring, Maryland, a suburb of Washington with large Jewish and immigrant populations, was particularly appealing to me. I liked the schools in Montgomery County; not only were they unusually well equipped, but they also placed special emphasis on the multicultural origin of their students.

I liked the large posters at the entrance announcing proudly: "We are from all over the world," welcoming everyone in different languages and scripts (*Schriften*). I liked the way in which teachers and secretaries assisted students while I discussed curricula, class schedules, special classes in English as a foreign language, music, and computer science. I liked the way in which students were able to come to their teachers with private questions and found an open ear. I noticed the caring tone in their voices; they were insignificant, almost banal conversations about normal problems of young students. The conversations were caring and affectionate. I could definitely see my children attending these schools. I was hoping that they would soon feel as at home there as the others seemed to.

The next step was to find an apartment in the vicinity of both schools. I asked friends to help me and also consulted an agency. I wanted a place in a large, high-rise building that would be children- and animal-friendly, so that every time my kids opened the door they would come into contact with foreigners, and every time they left the apartment they would meet other kids. I wanted a place with a swimming pool so that my children could spend the hot, humid summers outdoors, swimming and playing with others in a situation where they could feel comfortable without necessarily speaking the same language or perfect English. A place where they could make friends without having to search them out and would have a chance to see how other people lived without seeming too curious or intrusive. I could sit at the pool and work on my new book and also be there whenever my kids needed me. I wanted them to be integrated without having to make it a conscious effort.

On August 4th, 1994, I moved to the United States with my daughters and our Polish puppy. Everything had been carefully planned. But the move still turned out to be somewhat chaotic; Felix Kuballa and his camera team accompanied us to the U.S. They documented the final hectic days between the end of the school year in Passau and the remaining research I was doing for a book dealing with a gruesome massacre and the almost unbelievable rescue of 3,500 concentration camp prisoners in Nammering, a neighboring town of Passau. They were with us while we were packing our lives into boxes and suitcases and they were there when we said our good-byes to my parents in the Munich airport. All the other passengers had already boarded the plane when they were still interviewing us about what this move meant for us: the move from a small town in Lower Bavaria to a metropolis like Washington, D.C. They asked us about our expectations and our hopes. They asked if this would be a good-bye forever and if this was difficult for us.

We had not decided how long we would stay—perhaps for two, three years. We needed at least this much time to allow the children to learn a second language and to get used to a new culture, to let them get accustomed to a society about which they knew close to nothing. We would stay just long enough for them not to lose touch with their home, in case they ever decided to return and attend school in Germany. Then again, we might stay as long as eight or ten years, until they could complete high school, and then return at that point. It was certainly possible that one of the children might want to go back and I would stay in the U.S. with the other one. And, although it seemed highly unlikely, I didn't want to exclude the possibility that this move might indeed be final. For me the most important consideration were the wishes of my children, as long as they were living with me. All this remained to be seen.

When Felix Kuballa from the German television station, Westdeutscher Rundfunk (WDR) asked us what we were most looking forward to, each of us had a different answer: for me it was most of all freedom, in more ways than one, both professionally as well as privately. For the children it was mostly the new schools, new friends, and all the new animals that they wanted to experience in the wild.

Felix asked whether it was hard for us to leave. Nadine, who was twelve at the time, told him that she was happy to leave all this behind. Salome, who was nine, said that she would miss my parents and my brother and sister. For me the decision had been an easy one—even though I liked the idea of returning to Germany to visit some of my relatives.

We changed flights in Amsterdam and there was unfortunately no time to visit the Anne Frank House. I don't know how we would ever have managed to drag all our carry-on luggage through the airport without the help of the camera team. And all that waiting around in airports and standing in line at customs together created a bond between us. Suddenly we didn't just share theoretical, academic concerns, but some quite practical ones as well: when the children couldn't keep their eyes open any longer, the camera people had to stop filming; when some of our furniture was less delivered than simply deposited right inside our door in small pieces, they helped us assemble it. We girls didn't know the first thing about putting furniture together—nor did the dog. In turn we let them film the logistic disaster of the first few days; they filmed us when we arrived, completely worn out, standing in front of the White House; they filmed us walking the puppy outside the Capitol, eating hot dogs, and shopping at the supermarket—in what felt like tropical temperatures. They accompanied us when we visited the Holocaust Museum, where its director, Michael Berenbaum, had offered me a position as an associate researcher. They filmed Salome and Nadine at the pool making friends with other children. When the team left a few days later to return to Germany we had become so accustomed to their presence that we almost missed them.

But daily life kept us very busy: the children had to be signed up for classes, they needed some extra vaccinations, and they took a look at their new schools. At the end of August, summer vacation was over.

Salome wrote a letter to her grandmother and described how fascinated she was with the supermarket across the street and its huge assortment of goods. She visited it at least once or twice every day, just to explore: its many varieties of pasta, and the differences between the cash registers: one was only for cash payments, another one would accept no more than ten items, yet another one for check payments and one for wheelchair access; there was even one for children who weren't allowed to eat sweets and where no candy was displayed. Altogether, she discovered, there were fifteen different checkouts.

In the stores next door to the supermarket one could look at photos, buy an iguana, or take the dog along and pet baby rabbits. And sometimes there would even hold a small fair in the lot in front of the shops. Our puppy was the only one who had a hard time. Not only did he have to endure the nearly unbearable heat, he also had to stay on a leash all the time. In Passau he had lead a life of freedom. He was free to come and go as he pleased or even to run all over the neighborhood; every now and then we would run into him at the butcher shop where he could be found standing in line. In Washington he always had to be kept on a leash, he had to wait to go outside and do his business, and he lived on the eighth floor of an apartment building where he could chase squirrels only with his eyes, from his lookout point and on the balcony.

As far as I was concerned, my life had changed significantly as well: from now on I didn't have my parents there any longer to watch my children when I was traveling. I didn't have a sister nearby or a brother-in-law who would take the kids to spend a weekend with them in the countryside when I was busy with work. I didn't have my brother who would take his nieces for a ride on his motorcycle to explore the mountain paths, or simply for movies and ice cream. I didn't have my uncle or my Granny who loved to see us anytime and as often as they could. Now I had become what so many others had been before me: a single mother with two young daughters. I was busy lecturing and only a few weeks after moving to the U.S. I began to give talks at various universities and colleges about Passau and the Nazi era, about Germany and the neo-Nazis, about my work and the various reactions to it.

People would frequently recognize me and ask for autographs; they had seen the movie *The Nasty Girl* and wanted to tell me that they approved of what I was doing. Total strangers embraced me in the elevator, in the Metro, on the street, and in supermarkets. Some had seen me on *60 Minutes* and recognized my face. They welcomed me and told me how happy they were to know that I was here, in their country.

This wasn't entirely a new experience for me, but it certainly was for my daughters. They weren't used to this kind of attention at home. At first they reacted surprised, yet amused. They made jokes about how fortunate they felt to be able to see me every day. But eventually they got used to it. That was just the way it was here. I was relieved that it didn't go to their heads and that they accepted things nonchalantly.

One day when I opened the *Washington Post* I could hardly believe my eyes: "The Suppressed Murders in My Hometown," read the headline. *Suppressed Murders* . . . this was the title of my latest book. My first thought was: who was using my title here in Washington? I read it again and noticed that this was a big advertisement from the Holocaust Museum. They were announcing my lecture as well as the fact that I would receive the Conscience in Media Award by the American Society of Journalists and Authors. Everything happened very quickly after that. Primarily it was the Jewish organizations and German professors teaching at universities who wanted me to be a guest speaker at their departments. Before I knew it I was traveling all over the country to speak on the topic of *Zivilcourage*. It was the kind of courage that had been missing in so many people I had met in my life and also the kind of courage I had come to truly value in a few very special human beings. It had become very important for me to cultivate this quality in myself and to encourage it in young people, and I was ready and willing to invest as much time and energy as was needed to do so.

In order to make all this possible I would need a babysitter as well as a work permit. A lawyer who specialized in these kinds of cases was quickly able to arrange for a visa that suited me. She applied for a status as "Extraordinary Ability Alien," a designation which sounds truly alien, but which really means nothing more than the fact that I was a foreigner with special qualifications. A few weeks later the American government granted me this status without further complication. I received my green card, which granted me permanent residency status with all its rights and duties—but without, naturally, the right to vote.

The children, of course, would need a babysitter; according to Maryland law they were not allowed to be alone at home even for a few hours as long as the youngest one was not at least thirteen years old. On the first day of school, two African American women offered to take the job. I chose Terry, a beautiful young woman of twenty-six, who had two children herself. She lived one floor below us and her daughter Shauna already knew my daughters. Shauna took the bus to school with Salome, she loved our dog, and she had a pet boa constrictor. Whenever I had to go someplace, Terry took care of Salome, Nadine, and, of course, Misha the puppy; they did their homework together and they went shopping together. The children would spend the night at Terry's and she would walk them to the school bus in the morning. In the afternoon, when they came home, I was usually already back myself. With the exception of a few mishaps (such as Misha getting off his leash while being walked, Terry oversleeping, or her son having an asthma attack and being transported via helicopter to the children's hospital) everything was working out just fine. After two weeks Salome informed me that she wanted to learn Spanish: the Hispanics in the building and at school spoke Spanish to each other and she wanted to be able to share their language. This was more than I had expected. I was delighted. Salome was even prepared to attend extra classes twice a week and to get up an hour early. Terry picked her up and took her and Shauna to school: Shauna's father lived in New York and she had not seen him for years—he was Hispanic.

The orthodontist who had his practice across the street was fitting my children with braces; he was a Jew, of Polish descent, and had read all about me. The pediatrician next door was Hispanic, the dentist was a Jew of German descent, Salome's teacher was married to a Polish man who had survived in Germany as a forced laborer and was now was an acquisitions editor of non-fiction books at the Library of Congress. The librarian at the public library, who helped my children find materials about Haiti or Spanish language books for homework assignments, had seen *The Nasty Girl*. Wherever we went there were people who knew who I was and what I was doing. We were made to feel part of everything without ever having to try.

My life had not only changed for the better, it had also become much more stressful; as soon as the children left for school I went to work researching. I was constantly on the phone and faxes were coming in and going out non-stop. When the girls came home in the afternoons I helped them with their homework. I studied science and French with Nadine, Spanish with Salome, and English with both. I admit that I actually profited from all this and learned some things myself in the process: never before had I learned to translate English into French, Spanish into English, French into English, never had I learned (with the help of a crossword puzzle exercise) about the complex structures of human cells, nor had I ever constructed a model thereof out of seeds and half a tennis ball. My vocabulary and my knowledge were increasing almost daily!

At the end of September my twelve-year-old daughter wrote an enthusiastic letter to my mother:

Dear Granny!

It's been almost a month since I started at my new school. Even though my English wasn't very good when we got here I haven't really had any problems so far: the teachers are all very nice and used to foreigners. In the beginning I was in an English class for beginners, but after only three weeks I had gotten so good that I was able to skip a year. Now I'm with kids who have been in the States for at least three years, some of them even for five. It's a lot of fun. I have seven subjects and we have the same class schedule each day. The first lesson is World Studies, sort of like a combination of geography and history. Then we have PE. We play a new sport every six weeks. Right now we are learning to play tennis. It's amazing: each student has his own locker and afterwards we have to take a shower. The school gives us fresh towels. On Fridays we have to take our gym clothes home to have them washed. Which is good because they get very smelly. The third class is ESOL, or English for foreigners. There are children from all over the world at our school: from Bangladesh, Russia, Mexico, El Salvador, Korea, Japan, Cuba, and Cameroon. I'm the only one from Germany. Sometimes I feel like I must have lost my color somewhere, even if I have gotten really brown from playing in the sun.

Fourth period we have science: that includes biology, chemistry and physics all in one. I do at least one to two hours of homework every day. That makes Mommy really happy: if you thought it was hard for me, just imagine how long it takes her to get through everything. Sometimes I'm faster than she is. But we're both learning English together. The funniest thing is when Mom tries to explain things that we learned at school without having seen them herself. For example, the other day I had to write a report about a slug experiment, which involved a slug and a flashlight. I had to shine the flashlight on the slug and watch it to see what it would do, how many millimeters it would slither across a piece of sandpaper, where the slime trail was secreted from, how they breathe. . . . Do you want to come and help me out?

Fifth period is my favorite: math. Yes indeed! I'm the best student in the class (don't tell me "that's probably because the others are even worse than you are" like Grandpa once told Mommy).

Sixth period is music, specifically orchestra. Can you imagine what that sounds like? Lev, the Russian kid, for instance, had never touched a violin in his life before. . . . But soon we'll be having our first performance; I'll be wearing a black velvet skirt . . .

My last class is French. You probably think I'm not doing so well with my two years of French. But really, I'm getting straight "A's." If you think I'm making this up I can show you my report card.

I'd better go to bed now. I'll write again soon. After all, I want to have something left to tell you next time.

See ya soon, Nadine.

The children got used to our new life very quickly and I was both happy and relieved to see them thrive the way they did. When Felix Kuballa returned with his camera team to see how we were and to ask how life had changed for us, the children introduced him to our new "housemates": Nadine had bought a white rat and a python from the pet store in the mall next door and she was caring for them tenderly and attentively. She'd wear the snake like a necklace while she did her homework and had it wrapped around her arm as we went shopping. "Snakey" slept next to her bed at night. Misha was the only one who was jealous. Salome snuggled with her three white rats. A black cat would soon join the "family." And that's just the way it was in our house.

When Felix Kuballa asked the children if they were homesick they both laughed. "No," they said. They were fascinated by everything here, especially the schools. They told him how well they were treated and how helpful both the students and the teachers were, even though they hadn't understood things right away. Nadine said on camera that she wanted to stay in America forever and that one day she might even want to become an American citizen. At home, she said, she wouldn't like to be a foreigner, but here it was fine. She was treated with respect and consideration, so much more than she had expected. Salome agreed, and even though she was not quite as certain that she wanted to stay forever, she definitely wanted to be here for a very long time. She later wrote the following letter to my sister Gisela:

Silver Spring, October 1994
Dear Auntie,

I've been here now for two months. School is still a lot of fun. Soon I'll know as much about computers as you do. We have a lesson every Monday. There are nineteen children in my class with various skin colors—there's Mariya Kalinina from Russia, Choi won Choi from Korea, Eddie Saine from Cuba, and then there's Lenin Flores, Gabriela Navarotti, Allison Gariala, and Kevin Demoro—all Hispanics. Gabriela sits next to me. She and Allison help me the most. Can you imagine, Aunty, we're only in second grade and we're learning to use computers—isn't that great? We could never do that at home. But best of all is lunchtime. Yummy. Each day we get to choose between two kinds of meals, plus dessert of course. On Friday we'll get Pizza again. That's the best. On Halloween there's a special lunch for us "ghouls": roasted gravestones, grilled ghosts, and witches' brew . . . Are you scared yet? I can hardly wait! We get to run around and be wild. Except when we have visitors. If a grown-up is watching we quickly turn back into "angels." After lunch we get to go to the playground. Imagine something like that in Germany. Here all the schools have playgrounds and the students are actually allowed to use them! Most of the time we play a game called "tag," which is something like *Fangenspielen*, or "touch the person," or "chicken." But the rules are too complicated to explain in a letter. You'll just have to come and watch us, ok?

My favorite are the monkey bars; you can swing around on them while dangling on your arms upside down just like a monkey. Some of the kids here are really good at jump rope, using as many as three ropes all at once. I'll still have to practice before I'll let you watch me.

My favorite subject is ESOL, English for speakers of other languages. There are seven of us in that class: two African kids, one Hispanic, one Korean, two Russians and me. The one African is in the same grade as me, the Hispanic, the Russians, and the other African are in the fourth grade, and last but not least the Korean is in the third grade. The lessons are fun and we're all learning fast. Anytime we want to talk to each other we have to speak in English. Can you imagine? Our teacher shows us how to pronounce the words so that they sound right. It's really not that difficult. We all like each other, and I especially like the Korean girl and the Hispanic boy. They are a lot of fun and very smart.

That's all for now, Auntie,
I hope I see you soon, Salome.

As for myself, I was able to arrange my own work schedule, though I constantly had to contend with pressing deadlines. Wherever I was I had my laptop with me: in the taxi, at the airport, at the hairdresser's, or in the hotel. That way I managed to write about five pages per "event." I was working like a lunatic.

As much as I enjoyed participating in the various charity events, I still had my problems with so-called small receptions, where only select, "very important" guests were welcome. Some people paid up to $5,000 to be invited. I still avoid these events whenever I can. I have a hard time making the rounds and shaking hands or letting myself be embraced and kissed by total strangers, and I'm sometimes tired of hearing the same compliments over and over again. I dread being photographed again and again with various donors and to having to smile into dozens of cameras. And I don't enjoy signing autographs. Sometimes I wonder what good they really are to people. Occasionally people would touch me and say that they are taking the blessing home to their families. Such thinking is still completely foreign to me.

But now I've learned how things work in America. I know that this is a way for people to show respect to each other and to collect donations and so I do occasionally participate. I certainly don't want to hurt anybody's feelings.

Chapter 31

ONE HUNDRED FIFTY U.S. SOLDIERS IN PASSAU

In addition to various book projects I was hard at work with preparations for the 50th anniversary of Germany's liberation from National Socialism: I was determined to bring back to Passau and to Pocking as many liberators as possible. I knew that there had been four divisions that had played a major role: one was Russian and three were American. I had already been in contact with one of the American units and had applied to the City of Passau to arrange for a ceremony where they would be received as Guests of Honor (*Ehrengäste*) on May 3rd and be accommodated in a hotel for one night. They were mostly Jews and Christians. I'd also been in touch with E. G. McConnell, an African American who had been part of a famous African American Tank Battalion and I'd asked him to come to Pocking on May 2nd. I wanted him to speak about what it had meant back then to come to Germany as a black man with an opportunity to liberate white non-Nazis; and I wanted him to talk about what it was like to return to the United States and to see that it was mostly the white people who received military honors. . . . He immediately agreed to participate.

I still had to search for the third unit. With the Russian unit I was assisted, once again, by fate. A television crew from the international German news station Deutsche Welle was filming my presentation at the Holocaust Museum in Washington and the subsequent award ceremony. They still needed to fill in some gaps in their report and asked me to accompany them to the museum's research center, so they could film me doing some of my research. When we arrived they wanted me to walk toward the building's entrance for the camera. While the cameraman was setting up to get just the right angle and the soundman was arranging his equipment I saw three men and a woman exit through the revolving door. Two of the men were wearing uniforms; they were being photographed in front of the museum's memorial.

I was drawn toward the group. I recognized the Cyrillic characters on their epaulets. I excused myself for a moment and walked over to them. They seemed stiff and very official and were speaking a language I didn't understand a single word of. I asked them in English where they were from and the lady standing next to them answered that they were from Moscow. Moscow . . . Moscow! I was thrilled! Full of expectation and perhaps a bit obnoxiously I asked them if they could help me: I was searching for the few remaining Russian prisoners of war who had survived in my former hometown. (Of course I knew that most of the people who had survived the war and had escaped the massacre in Passau were shot by the Russians as soon as they crossed the Czech border. But I thought it wouldn't hurt the Russians to do a little thinking about their own past, either). I told them that I was from Germany and that I'd like to talk with them and see some of their photographs. I also mentioned that I would very much like to bring back, on May 2nd, some of the other victims from back then. I also wanted to bring back some of the Russian veterans who had entered just a few kilometers outside the city limits of my former hometown in April and May 1945. Both men were listening attentively but remained silent. The lady was translating my words into Russian, and as our conversation went on they began to nod in appreciation. They told me that it was indeed very difficult to find former prisoners of war, particularly since the collapse of the Soviet Union. It was questionable as well whether there were any remaining soldiers from that unit to be found. There was a better chance of coming up with the names of the veterans. The translator also confided in me who these men actually were: one of them was the director of a museum dedicated to the Second World War; he intended to design a museum similar to the Holocaust Museum in Washington D.C. The other one was working on the projects dealing with veterans.

We exchanged business cards, upon which the fourth man told me that of course he knew who I was and what I was working to accomplish. He had read *Wintergreen—Suppressed Murders* and he had seen me on *60 Minutes*. He had also visited Passau and he was a historian.

At my next speech in Detroit I decided to add a request at the end: anyone who might be able to assist me with the project of bringing back those people, should please come forward. It was impossible for me to do it alone. Ever since I've had to ask for money, to allow me to invite as many people as possible. Because one thing seems certain: my hometown would neither finance nor organize these kinds of events. Yet I also knew that the *Oberbürgermeister* and the city councilmen (*Stadträte*) would now show enough tact to at least extend official invitations to all these guests, and to make it possible for them to experience what they longed for: to be warmly welcomed back this time, to be invited back as *Ehrengäste* and to hear the simple words: "Thank You."

In October the City approved my application to offer these guests an invitation to participate in a three-river cruise and an organ concert. I was hoping that the bishop would agree, together with a rabbi and a Lutheran minister, to hold an inter-faith commemorative service at the Cathedral. I had originally asked for this the previous summer. The veterans were looking forward to it, and whatever it would take for me as a private citizen to make sure this would happen, I was going to do it.

I also would see to it that the few survivors of our concentration sub-camps would be received as *Ehrengäste* and that they would witness the building of a museum dedicated to the memory of their suffering. There was no doubt that this kind of undertaking would be difficult: not only would I have to search for, order, and pay for all the relevant documents myself, I'd also have to supervise the organization of the exhibit, arrange for someone to give tours and to publicize the event. But it was definitely worth the effort.

■   ■   ■

Fifty years after the Second World War, a group of more than two hundred U.S. veterans and survivors from the local concentration camps returned to the sites in and near Passau where they had first been brought together. There they commemorated the dead and testified to what they had witnessed.

Occurring more than half a century after the fact, all of this was belated, to be sure. It was also necessary. I personally had no illusions about what this gesture might ultimately accomplish. I knew that no matter how hard I might try, I could not undo a single one of those horrible memories nor could I heal the wounds that had been inflicted. As a private citizen, I would never be able to change the people around me or liberate them from their careless attitudes. All I could do was offer small symbolic gestures of one individual's good will. As a young German, I don't see this as an opportunity, I consider it an obligation.

Incredibly there were still many in Passau who felt insulted by the presence of American soldiers and did not call them liberators, but occupiers and enemies. I, on the other hand, have vowed to meet with American veterans whenever and wherever I have the opportunity, because I am well

aware of how much we all owe them. It was not just a "duty" they performed back then; it was not just an obligation they fulfilled. They made
a difference, and not just to their fellow Americans. One of the greatest
honors I would ever receive would be a document stating that the 65th
Infantry Division of General Patton's legendary Third Army had elected
me an honorary member. The official reason given was that I had managed to help complete what they had begun half a century earlier:

The liberation process.